THE GREAT CANON

The Work
of
Saint Andrew of Crete

T0164202

HOLY TRINITY PUBLICATIONS
THE PRINTSHOP OF ST. JOB OF POCHAEV
Holy Trinity Monastery
Jordanville, New York

Printed with the blessing of His Eminence,
Metropolitan Hilarion, First Hierarch
of the Russian Orthodox Church Outside of Russia

Compilation: The Great Canon © 2016 Holy Trinity Monastery
Text: The Great Canon by St. Andrew of Crete © 1977 Kallistos Ware
Text: The Life of St Mary of Egypt © 2005 Holy Trinity Monastery

PRINTSHOP OF
SAINT JOB OF POCHAEV

An imprint of

HOLY TRINITY PUBLICATIONS
Holy Trinity Monastery
Jordanville, New York 13361-0036
www.holytrinitypublications.com

ISBN: 978–0-88465–452–0 (Paperback)
ISBN: 978–0-88465-424-7 (Epub)
ISBN: 978–0-88465-458-2 (Mobipocket)

Library of Congress Control Number 2016961452

Third Printing 2020

Contents

The Great Canon

THE WORK OF SAINT ANDREW OF CRETE.

Monday of the First Week

On Monday of the first week of Lent, the Canon is chanted during Great Compline, immediately following Psalm 69. The Eirmoi are sung twice at the beginning of each ode. Only at the Ninth Ode is the Eirmos repeated at the end, in place of "It is truly meet." Before each Troparion we make the sign of the Cross and bow three times.

Ode 1 · Tone 6

EIRMOS: *He is for me unto salvation Helper and Protector. He is my God and I glorify Him, God of my fathers is He and I exalt Him, for He is greatly glorified.*

REFRAIN: *Have mercy on me, O God, have mercy on me.*

Where shall I begin to weep for the actions of my wretched life? What first-fruit shall I offer, O Christ, in this my lamentation? But in Thy compassion grant me forgiveness of sins.

Come, wretched soul, with thy flesh to the Creator of all. Make confession to Him, and abstain henceforth from thy past brutishness; and offer to God tears of repentance.

I have rivalled in transgression Adam the first-formed man, and I have found myself stripped naked of God, of the eternal Kingdom and its joy, because of my sins.[1]

[1] Gen 3: 7–11.

Woe to thee, miserable soul! How like thou art to the first Eve! For thou hast looked in wickedness and wast grievously wounded; thou hast touched the tree and rashly tasted the deceptive food.[2]

Instead of the visible Eve, I have the Eve of the mind: the passionate thought in my flesh, showing me what seems sweet; yet whenever I taste from it, I find it bitter.[3]

Adam was justly banished from Eden because he disobeyed one commandment of Thine, O Saviour. What then shall I suffer, for I am always rejecting Thy words of life?[4]

Glory to the Father, and to the Son, and to the Holy Spirit.

Trinity beyond all being, worshipped in Unity, take from me the heavy yoke of sin, and in Thy compassion grant me tears of compunction.

Both now and ever, and unto the ages of ages. Amen.

O Theotokos, the hope and protection of those who sing thy praises, take from me the heavy yoke of sin and, pure Lady, accept me in repentance.

Ode 2

EIRMOS: *Attend, O heaven, and I shall speak and sing in praise of Christ, who took flesh from a Virgin and came to dwell among us.*

REFRAIN: *Have mercy on me, O God, have mercy on me.*

Attend, O heaven, and I shall speak; give ear, O earth, to the voice of one who repents before God and sings His praise.[5]

Look upon me, God my Saviour, with Thy merciful eye, and accept my fervent confession.

More than all men have I sinned; I alone have sinned against Thee. But as God take pity on Thy creation, O Saviour.

With my lustful desires I have formed within myself the deformity of the passions and disfigured the beauty of my mind.

I am surrounded by the storm of sin, O compassionate Lord. But stretch out Thine hand to me, as once Thou hast to Peter.[6]

I have stained the garment of my flesh, O Saviour, and defiled that which was made in Thine image and likeness.

---

[2]Gen. 3: 6.   [3]Gen. 3: 6.   [4]Gen. 3: 23; Acts 7: 38.
[5]Deut. 32: 1.   [6]Matt. 14. 31.

With the lusts of passion I have darkened the beauty of my soul, and turned my whole mind entirely into dust.

I have torn the first garment that the Creator wove for me in the beginning, and now I lie naked.[7]

I have clothed myself in the torn coat that the serpent wove for me by his counsel, and I am ashamed.

I offer to Thee, O merciful Lord, the tears of the Harlot. Take pity on me, O Saviour, in Thy compassion.[8]

I looked upon the beauty of the tree and my mind was deceived; and now I lie naked and ashamed.[9]

All the ruling passions have ploughed upon my back, making long furrows of wickedness.[10]

Glory to the Father, and to the Son, and to the Holy Spirit.

I sing Thy praises, One in Three Persons, God of all, Father, Son and Holy Spirit.

Both now and ever, and unto the ages of ages. Amen.

O Theotokos undefiled, Virgin alone worthy of all praise, intercede fervently for our salvation.

Ode 3

EIRMOS: *Upon the unshaken rock of Thy commandments, O Christ, make firm Thy Church.*

REFRAIN: *Have mercy on me, O God, have mercy on me.*

The Lord once rained down fire from heaven and consumed the land of Sodom.[11]

O my soul, flee like Lot to the mountain, and take refuge in Zoar before it is too late.[12]

Flee from the flames, my soul, flee from the burning heat of Sodom, flee from destruction by the fire of God.[13]

I alone have sinned against Thee, I have sinned more than all men; reject me not, O Christ my Saviour.

Thou art the Good Shepherd: seek me, the lamb that has strayed, and do not forget me.[14]

---

[7]Gen. 3: 7.　[8]Lk. 7: 38.　[9]Gen. 3: 6–7.　[10]Ps. 128: 3.　[11]Gen. 19: 24.
[12]Gen. 19: 22.　[13]Deut. 4: 24; Heb. 12: 29.　[14]Jn. 10: 11; Lk. 15: 4–6.

Thou art my beloved Jesus, Thou art my Creator; in Thee shall I be justified, O Saviour.

I confess to Thee, O Saviour: I have sinned against Thee without measure. But in Thy compassion absolve and forgive me.

Glory to the Father, and to the Son, and to the Holy Spirit.

O God, Trinity in Unity, save us from error and temptation and distress.

Both now and ever, and unto the ages of ages. Amen.

Hail, Womb that held God! Hail, Throne of the Lord! Hail, Mother of our life!

Ode 4

EIRMOS: *The Prophet heard of Thy coming, O Lord, and he was afraid: how Thou wast to be born of a Virgin and revealed to men, and he said: 'I have heard the report of Thee and I was afraid.' Glory to Thy power, O Lord.*

REFRAIN: *Have mercy on me, O God, have mercy on me.*

O righteous Judge, despise not Thy works; forsake not Thy creation. I have sinned as a man, I alone, more than any other man, O Thou who lovest mankind. But as Lord of all Thou hast the power to pardon sins.[15]

The end draws near, my soul, the end draws near; yet thou dost not care or make ready. The time grows short, rise up: the Judge is at the door. The days of our life pass swiftly, as a dream, as a flower. Why do we trouble ourselves in vain?[16]

Awake, my soul, consider the actions which thou hast done; set them before thine eyes, and let the drops of thy tears fall. With boldness tell Christ of thy deeds and thoughts, and so be justified.

No sin has there been in life, no evil deed, no wickedness, that I have not committed, O Saviour. I have sinned as no one ever before, in mind, word and intent, in disposition, thought and act.

For this I am condemned in my misery, for this I am convicted by the verdict of my own conscience, which is more compelling than all else in the world. O my Judge and Redeemer, who knowest my heart, spare and deliver and save me in my wretchedness.

[15]Mk. 2: 10.   [16]Matt. 24: 33; Ps. 38: 7.

The ladder which the great Patriarch Jacob saw of old is an example, O my soul, of approach through action and of ascent in knowledge. If then thou dost wish to live rightly in action and knowledge and contemplation, be thou made new.[17]

In privation Jacob the Patriarch endured the burning heat by day and the frost by night, making daily gains of sheep and cattle, shepherding, wrestling and serving, to win his two wives.[18]

By the two wives, understand action and knowledge in contemplation. Leah is action, for she had many children; and Rachel is knowledge, for she endured great toil. For without toil, O my soul, neither action nor contemplation will succeed.

Glory to the Father, and to the Son, and to the Holy Spirit.

Undivided in Essence, unconfused in Persons, I confess Thee as God: Triune Deity, one in kingship and throne; and to Thee I raise the great thrice-holy hymn that is sung on high.[19]

Both now and ever, and unto the ages of ages. Amen.

Thou givest birth and art a virgin, and in both thou remainest by nature inviolate. He who is born makes new the laws of nature, and the womb brings forth without travail. When God so wills, the natural order is overcome; for He does whatever He wishes.

Ode 5

EIRMOS: *From the night I seek Thee early, O Lover of mankind: give me light, I pray Thee, and guide me in Thy commandments, and teach me, O Saviour, to do Thy will.*

REFRAIN: *Have mercy on me, O God, have mercy on me.*

In night have I passed all my life: for the night of sin has covered me with darkness and thick mist. But make me, O Saviour, a son of the day.[20]

In my misery I have followed Reuben's example, and have devised a wicked and unlawful plan against the most high God, defiling my bed as he defiled his father's.[21]

I confess to Thee, O Christ my King: I have sinned, I have sinned like the brethren of Joseph, who once sold the fruit of purity and chastity.[22]

---

[17]Gen. 28: 12.   [18]Gen. 29: 16–30; 30: 31–3; 31: 38–41.   [19]Isa. 6: 3; Rev. 4: 8.
[20]Eph. 5: 8; 1 Thess. 5: 5.   [21]Gen. 35: 22: 49: 4.   [22]Gen. 37: 27–28.

As a figure of the Lord, O my soul, the righteous and gentle Joseph was sold into bondage by his brethren; but thou hast sold thyself entirely to thy sins.

O miserable and wicked soul, imitate the righteous and pure mind of Joseph; and do not live in wantonness, sinfully indulging thy disordered desires.[23]

Once Joseph was cast into a pit, O Lord and Master, as a figure of Thy Burial and Resurrection. But what offering such as this shall I ever make to Thee?[24]

Glory to the Father, and to the Son, and to the Holy Spirit.

We glorify Thee, O Trinity, the one God. Holy, holy, holy, art Thou: Father, Son and Spirit, simple Essence and Unity, worshipped for ever.

Both now and ever, and unto the ages of ages. Amen.

O Virgin inviolate and Mother who hast not known man, from thee has God, the Creator of the ages, taken human flesh, uniting to Himself the nature of men.

Ode 6

EIRMOS: *With my whole heart I cried to the all-compassionate God: and He heard me from the lowest depths of hell, and brought my life out of corruption.*

REFRAIN: *Have mercy on me, O God, have mercy on me.*

I offer to Thee in purity, O Saviour, the tears of mine eyes and groanings from the depths of my heart, crying: 'I have sinned against Thee, O God; be merciful to me.'[25]

Like Dathan and Abiram, O my soul, thou hast become a stranger to Thy Lord; but from the lowest depth of hell cry out, 'Spare me', that the earth may not open and swallow thee up.[26]

Raging as a maddened heifer, O my soul, thou art become like Ephraim. As a hart from the nets rescue then thy life, gaining wings through action and the mind's contemplation.[27]

O my soul, the hand of Moses shall be our assurance, proving how God can cleanse a life full of leprosy and make it white as snow. So do not despair of thyself, though thou art leprous.[28]

---

[23]Gen. 39: 7–20.   [24]Gen. 37:24.   [25]Lk. 18: 13.
[26]Num. 16:32.   [27]Hos. 10:11.   [28]Ex. 4: 6–8..

Glory to the Father, and to the Son, and to the Holy Spirit.

'I am the Trinity, simple and undivided, yet divided in Persons, and I am the Unity, by Nature one', says the Father and the Son and the divine Spirit.

Both now and ever, and unto the ages of ages. Amen.

Thy womb bore God for us, fashioned in our shape. O Theotokos, pray to Him as the Creator of all, that we may be justified through thine intercessions.

Lord, have mercy. *Thrice.* Glory . . . Both Now . . .

KONTAKION · TONE 6

My soul, O my soul, rise up! Why art thou sleeping? The end draws near and soon thou shalt be troubled. Watch, then, that Christ thy God may spare thee, for He is everywhere present and fills all things.

Ode 7

EIRMOS: *We have sinned, we have transgressed, we have done evil in Thy sight; we have not kept or followed Thy commandments. But reject us not utterly, O God of our fathers.*

REFRAIN: *Have mercy on me, O God, have mercy on me.*

I have sinned, I have offended, and I have set aside Thy commandments, for in sins have I progressed, and to my sores I have added wounds. But in Thy compassion have mercy upon me, O God of our fathers.

The secrets of my heart have I confessed to Thee, my Judge. See my abasement, see my affliction, and attend to my judgement now; and in Thy compassion have mercy upon me, O God of our fathers.

When Saul once lost his father's asses, in searching for them he found himself proclaimed as king. But watch, my soul, lest unknown to thyself thou prefer thine animal appetites to the Kingdom of Christ.[29]

David, the forefather of God, once sinned doubly, pierced with the arrow of adultery and the spear of murder. But thou, my soul, art more gravely sick than he, for worse than any acts are the impulses of thy will.[30]

David once joined sin to sin, adding murder to fornication; yet then he showed at once a twofold repentance. But thou, my soul, hast done worse things than he, yet thou hast not repented before God.[31]

[29]1 Kgs. [1 Sam.] 9: 3; 10: 1–2.   [30]2 Kgs. [2 Sam.] 11: 2–17.   [31]2 Kgs. [2 Sam.] 12: 13.

David once composed a hymn, setting forth, as in an ikon, the action he had done; and he condemned it, crying: 'Have mercy upon me, for against Thee only have I sinned, O God of all. Do Thou cleanse me.'[32]

Glory to the Father, and to the Son, and to the Holy Spirit.

O simple and undivided Trinity, O holy and consubstantial Unity: Thou art praised as Light and Lights, one Holy and three Holies. Sing, O my soul, and glorify Life and Lives, the God of all.

Both now and ever, and unto the ages of ages. Amen.

We praise thee, we bless thee, we venerate thee, O Mother of God: for thou hast given birth to One of the undivided Trinity, thy Son and God; and thou hast opened the heavenly places to us on earth.

Ode 8

EIRMOS: *The hosts of heaven give Him glory; before Him tremble cherubim and seraphim; let everything that has breath and all creation praise Him, bless Him, and exalt Him above all for ever.*

REFRAIN: *Have mercy on me, O God, have mercy on me.*

I have sinned, O Saviour, have mercy on me. Awaken my mind and turn me back; accept me in repentance and take pity on me as I cry: I have sinned against Thee, save me; I have done evil, have mercy on me.

Riding in the chariot of the virtues, Elijah was lifted up to heaven, high above earthly things. Reflect, O my soul, on his ascent.[33]

Elisha once took up the mantle of Elijah, and received a double portion of grace from the Lord: but in this grace, my soul, thou hast no share, by reason of thy greed and uncontrolled desires.[34]

With the mantle of Elijah, Elisha made the stream of Jordan stand still on either side: but in this grace, my soul, thou hast no share, by reason of thy greed and uncontrolled desires.[35]

The Shunammite woman gladly entertained the righteous Prophet: but in thy house, my soul, thou hast not welcomed stranger or traveller; and so thou shalt be cast out weeping from the bridal chamber.[36]

---

[32]Ps. 50: 3, 6, 11.   [33]4 [2] Kgs. 2: 11.   [34]4 [2] Kgs. 2: 9, 13.
[35]4 [2] Kgs. 2: 14.   [36]4 [2] Kgs. 4: 8; Matt. 22: 11–13.

O wretched soul, always thou hast imitated the unclean thoughts of Gehazi. Cast from thee, at least in thine old age, his love of money. Flee from the fire of hell, turning away from thy wickedness.[37]

Glory to the Father, and to the Son, and to the Holy Spirit.

Father without beginning, coeternal Son, and loving Comforter, the Spirit of righteousness; Begetter of the Word of God, Word of the Eternal Father, Spirit living and creative: O Trinity in Unity, have mercy on me.

Both now and ever, and unto the ages of ages. Amen.

As from purple silk, O undefiled Virgin, the spiritual robe of Emmanuel, His flesh, was woven in thy womb. Therefore we honour thee as Theotokos in very truth.

Ode 9

EIRMOS: *Conception without seed; nativity past understanding, from a Mother who never knew a man; childbearing undefiled. For the birth of God makes both natures new. Therefore, as Bride and Mother of God, with true worship all generations magnify thee.*

REFRAIN: *Have mercy on me, O God, have mercy on me.*

My mind is wounded, my body has grown feeble, my spirit is sick, my speech has lost its power, my life is dead; the end is at the door. What shalt thou do, then, miserable soul, when the Judge comes to examine thy deeds?

I have put before thee, my soul, Moses' account of the creation of the world, and after that all the recognized Scriptures that tell thee the story of the righteous and the wicked. But thou, my soul, hast followed the second of these, not the first, and hast sinned against God.

The Law is powerless, the Gospel of no effect, and the whole of Scripture is ignored by thee; the prophets and all the words of the righteous are useless. Thy wounds, my soul, have been multiplied, and there is no physician to heal thee.

I bring thee, O my soul, examples from the New Testament, to lead thee to compunction. Follow the example of the righteous, turn away from the sinful, and through prayers and fasting, through chastity and reverence, win back Christ's mercy.

---

[37] 4 [2] Kgs. 5: 21–7.

Christ became man, calling to repentance thieves and harlots. Repent, my soul: the door of the Kingdom is already open, and pharisees and publicans and adulterers pass through it before thee, changing their life.[38]

Christ became man and shared in my flesh; and willingly He performed all that belongs to my nature, only without sin. He set before thee, my soul, an example and image of His condescension.[39]

Christ saved the Wise Men and called the Shepherds; He revealed as martyrs a multitude of young children; He glorified the Elder and the aged Widow. But thou, my soul, hast not followed their lives and actions. Woe to thee when thou art judged![40]

The Lord fasted forty days in the wilderness, and at the end of them He was hungry, thus showing that He is man. Do not be dismayed, my soul! If the enemy attacks thee, through prayer and fasting drive him away.[41]

Glory to the Father, and to the Son, and to the Holy Spirit.

Let us glorify the Father, let us exalt the Son, and with faith let us worship the Spirit of God, undivided Trinity and Unity in essence. Let us adore Light and Lights, Life and Lives, giving light and life to the ends of the earth.

Both now and ever, and unto the ages of ages. Amen.

Watch over thy City, all-pure Mother of God. For by thee she reigns in faith, by thee she is made strong; by thee she is victorious, putting to flight every temptation, despoiling the enemy and ruling her subjects.

REFRAIN: *Holy father Andrew, pray to God for us.*

Venerable Andrew, father thrice-blessed, shepherd of Crete, cease not to offer prayer for us who sing thy praises; that we may be delivered from all danger and distress, from corruption and sin, who honour thy memory with faith.

AND AGAIN THE EIRMOS: *Conception without seed; nativity past understanding, from a Mother who never knew a man; childbearing undefiled. For the birth of God makes both natures new. Therefore, as Bride and Mother of God, with true worship all generations magnify thee.*

THEN THE REST OF GREAT COMPLINE

[38]Matt. 9: 13; 21: 31; Luke 15: 1.   [39]Heb. 4: 15.
[40]Matt. 2: 12; Lk. 2: 9–12; Matt. 2: 16; Lk. 2: 25–38.   [41]Matt. 4: 2; 17: 21.

Tuesday of the First Week

On Tuesday of the first week of Lent, the Canon is chanted during Great Compline, immediately following Psalm 69. The Eirmoi are sung twice at the beginning of each ode. Only at the Ninth Ode is the Eirmos repeated at the end, in place of "It is truly meet." Before each Troparion we make the sign of the Cross and bow three times.

Ode 1 · Tone 6

EIRMOS: *He is for me unto salvation Helper and Protector. He is my God and I glorify Him, God of my fathers is He and I exalt Him, for He is greatly glorified.*

REFRAIN: *Have mercy on me, O God, have mercy on me.*

By my own free choice have I incurred the guilt of Cain's murder. I have killed my conscience, bringing the flesh to life and making war upon the soul by my wicked actions.[1]

O Jesus, I have not been like Abel in his righteousness. Never have I offered Thee acceptable gifts or godly actions, a pure sacrifice or an unblemished life.[2]

Like Cain, O miserable soul, we too have offered, to the Creator of all, defiled actions and a polluted sacrifice and a worthless life: and so we also are condemned.[3]

As the potter moulds the clay, Thou hast fashioned me, giving me flesh and bones, breath and life. But accept me in repentance, O my Maker and Deliverer and Judge.[4]

I confess to Thee, O Saviour, the sins I have committed, the wounds of my soul and body, which murderous thoughts, like thieves, have inflicted inwardly upon me.[5]

Though I have sinned, O Saviour, yet I know that Thou art full of loving-kindness. Thou dost chastise with mercy and art fervent in compassion. Thou dost see me weeping and dost run to meet me, like the Father calling back the Prodigal Son.[6]

[1]Gen. 4:8.   [2]Gen. 4:4.   [3]Gen. 4:5.
[4]Gen. 2:7; Jer. 18:1–10; Rom. 9:21.   [5]Lk. 10:30.   [6]Lk. 15:20.

Glory to the Father, and to the Son, and to the Holy Spirit.

Trinity beyond all being, worshipped in Unity, take from me the heavy yoke of sin, and in Thy compassion grant me tears of compunction.

Both now and ever, and unto the ages of ages. Amen.

O Theotokos, the hope and protection of those who sing thy praises, take from me the heavy yoke of sin and, pure Lady, accept me in repentance.

Ode 2

EIRMOS: *Attend, O heaven, and I shall speak and sing in praise of Christ, who took flesh from a Virgin and came to dwell among us.*

REFRAIN: *Have mercy on me, O God, have mercy on me.*

Sin has stripped me of the robe that God once wove for me, and it has sewed for me garments of skin.[7]

I am clothed with the raiment of shame as with fig leaves, in condemnation of my self-willed passions.[8]

I am clad in a garment that is defiled and shamefully bloodstained by a life of passion and self-indulgence.

I have fallen beneath the painful burden of the passions and the corruption of material things; and I am hard pressed by the enemy.

Instead of freedom from possessions, O Saviour, I have pursued a life in love with material things, and now I wear a heavy yoke.

I have adorned the idol of my flesh with a many-coloured coat of shameful thoughts, and I am condemned.

I have cared only for the outward adornment, and neglected that which is within —the tabernacle fashioned by God.

I have discoloured with the passions the first beauty of the image, O Saviour. But seek me, as once Thou hast sought the lost coin, and find me.[9]

Like the Harlot I cry to Thee: I have sinned, I alone have sinned against Thee. Accept my tears also as sweet ointment, O Saviour.[10]

Like the Publican I cry to Thee: Be merciful, O Saviour, be merciful to me. For no child of Adam has ever sinned against Thee as I have sinned.[11]

Glory to the Father, and to the Son, and to the Holy Spirit.

I sing Thy praises, One in three Persons, God of all, Father, Son and Holy Spirit.

[7]Gen. 3:21.   [8]Gen. 3: 7.   [9]Lk. 15:8.   [10]Lk. 7:37–50.   [11]Lk. 18:13.

Both now and ever, and unto the ages of ages. Amen.

O Theotokos undefiled, Virgin alone worthy of all praise, intercede fervently for our salvation.

Ode 3

EIRMOS: *O Lord, upon the rock of Thy commandments make firm my wavering heart, for Thou alone art Holy and Lord.*

REFRAIN: *Have mercy on me, O God, have mercy on me.*

For me Thou art the Fountain of life and the Destroyer of death; and from my heart I cry to Thee before the end: I have sinned, be merciful to me and save me.[12]

I have sinned, O Lord, I have sinned against Thee; be merciful to me. For there is no sinner whom I have not surpassed in my offences.

I have followed the example, O Saviour, of those who lived in wantonness in the days of Noah; and like them I am condemned to drown in the flood.[13]

O my soul, thou hast followed Ham, who mocked his father. Thou hast not covered thy neighbour's shame, walking backwards with averted face.[14]

Flee, my soul, like Lot from the burning of sin; flee from Sodom and Gomorrah; flee from the flame of every brutish desire.[15]

Have mercy, O Lord, have mercy on me, I cry to Thee, when Thou comest with Thine angels to give to every man due return for his deeds.

Glory to the Father, and to the Son, and to the Holy Spirit.

O simple Unity praised in Trinity of Persons, uncreated Nature without beginning, save us who in faith worship Thy power.

Both now and ever, and unto the ages of ages. Amen.

O Mother of God, without knowing man thou hast given birth within time to the Son, who was begotten outside time from the Father; and, strange wonder! thou givest suck while still remaining Virgin.

---

[12]Ps. 35: 10; Jn. 4: 14; 7: 37.   [13]Gen. 6: 5–13; Matt. 24:37–39.
[14]Gen. 9:20–27.   [15]Gen. 19: 17–25.

Ode 4

EIRMOS: *The prophet heard of Thy coming, O Lord, and he was afraid: how Thou wast to be born of a Virgin and revealed to men, and he said: 'I have heard the report of Thee and I was afraid.' Glory to Thy power, O Lord.*

REFRAIN: *Have mercy on me, O God, have mercy on me.*

Be watchful, O my soul, be full of courage like Jacob the great Patriarch, that thou mayest acquire action with knowledge, and be named Israel, 'the mind that sees God'; so shalt thou reach by contemplation the innermost darkness and gain great merchandise.[16]

The great Patriarch had the twelve Patriarchs as children, and so he mystically established for thee, my soul, a ladder of ascent through action, in his wisdom setting his children as steps, by which thou canst mount upwards.[17]

Thou hast rivalled Esau the hated, O my soul, and given the birthright of thy first beauty to the supplanter; thou hast lost thy father's blessing and in thy wretchedness been twice supplanted, in action and in knowledge. Therefore repent now.[18]

Esau was called Edom because of his raging love for women; burning always with unrestrained desires and stained with sensual pleasure, he was named 'Edom', which means the red heat of a soul that loves sin.[19]

Thou hast heard, O my soul, of Job justified on a dung-hill, but thou hast not imitated his fortitude. In all thine experiences and trials and temptations, thou hast not kept firmly to thy purpose but hast proved inconstant.[20]

Once he sat upon a throne, but now he sits upon a dung-hill, naked and covered with sores. Once he was blessed with many children and admired by all, but suddenly he is childless and homeless. Yet he counted the dung-hill as a palace and his sores as pearls.

Glory to the Father, and to the Son, and to the Holy Spirit.

Undivided in Essence, unconfused in Persons, I confess Thee as God: Triune Deity, one in kingship and throne; and to Thee I raise the great thrice-holy hymn that is sung on high.[21]

Both now and ever, and unto the ages of ages. Amen.

---

[16]Gen. 32:28–30.   [17]Gen. 28: 12–14; 35: 22.   [18]Gen. 25:31–33; 27:36.
[19]Gen. 25:30.   [20]Job 2: 8–10.   [21]Isa. 6:3; Rev. 4:8..

Thou givest birth and art a virgin, and in both thou remainest by nature inviolate. He who is born makes new the laws of nature, and the womb brings forth without travail. When God so wills, the natural order is overcome; for He does whatever He wishes.

Ode 5

EIRMOS: *From the night I seek Thee early, O Lover of mankind: give me light, I pray Thee, and guide me in Thy commandments, and teach me, O Saviour, to do Thy will.*

REFRAIN: *Have mercy on me, O God, have mercy on me.*

Thou hast heard, my soul, of the basket of Moses: how he was borne on the waves of the river as if in a shrine; and so he avoided the bitter execution of Pharaoh's decree.[22]

Thou hast heard, wretched soul, of the midwives who once killed in its infancy the manly action of self-control: like great Moses, then, be suckled on wisdom.[23]

O miserable soul, thou hast not struck and killed the Egyptian mind, as did Moses the great. Tell me, then, how wilt thou go to dwell through repentance in the wilderness empty of passions?[24]

Moses the great went to dwell in the desert. Come, seek to follow his way of life, my soul, that in contemplation thou mayest attain the vision of God in the bush.[25]

Picture to thyself, my soul, the rod of Moses striking the sea and making hard the deep by the sign of the Holy Cross. Through the Cross thou also canst do great things.[26]

Aaron offered to God fire that was blameless and undefiled, but Hophni and Phinehas brought to Him, as thou hast done, my soul, strange fire and a polluted life.[27]

Glory to the Father and to the Son, and to the Holy Spirit.

We glorify Thee, O Trinity, the one God. Holy, holy, holy, art Thou: Father, Son and Spirit, simple Essence and Unity, worshipped for ever.

Both now and ever, and unto the ages of ages. Amen.

---

[22]Ex. 1:22–2:3.   [23]Ex. 1:16; 2–9.   [24]Ex. 2:12.
[25]Ex. 3:1–6.   [26]Ex. 14:16.   [27]Num. 16:1–40; 1 Kgs. [1Sam.]2:12–34.

O Virgin inviolate and Mother who hast not known man, from thee has God, the Creator of the ages, taken human flesh, uniting to Himself the nature of men.

Ode 6

EIRMOS: *With my whole heart I cried to the all-compassionate God: and He heard me from the lowest depths of hell, and brought my life out of corruption.*

REFRAIN: *Have mercy on me, O God, have mercy on me.*

The waves of my sins, O Saviour, have returned and suddenly engulfed me, as the waters of the Red Sea engulfed the Egyptians of old and their charioteers.[28]

Like Israel before thee, thou hast made a foolish choice, my soul; instead of the divine manna thou hast senselessly preferred the pleasure-loving gluttony of the passions.[29]

O my soul, thou hast valued the wells of Canaanite thoughts more than the veined Rock, Jesus, the Fountain of Wisdom from which flow the rivers of divine knowledge.[30]

The swine's meat, the flesh-pots and the food of Egypt thou hast preferred, my soul, to the food of heaven, as the ungrateful people did of old in the wilderness.[31]

When Thy servant Moses struck the rock with his rod, he prefigured Thy life-giving side, O Saviour, from which we all draw the water of life.[32]

Like Joshua the son of Nun, search and spy out, my soul, the land of thine inheritance and take up thy dwelling within it, through obedience to the law.[33]

Glory to the Father, and to the Son, and to the Holy Spirit.

'I am the Trinity, simple and undivided, yet divided in Persons, and I am the Unity, by Nature one', says the Father and the Son and the divine Spirit.

Both now and ever, and unto the ages of ages. Amen.

Thy womb bore God for us, fashioned in our shape. O Theotokos, pray to Him as the Creator of all, that we may be justified through thine intercessions.

[28]Ex. 14: 21–8.   [29]Ex 16:15; Num. 21: 5.
[30]Ex. 17:6. Num. 20:8; 2 Kgs. [2Sam.] 22:2; 1 Cor. 10:4.   [31]Ex. 16:3; Num. 11:4–7.
[32]Ex. 17:6; Num. 20:8; Jn. 19:34; 1 Cor. 10:4.   [33]Num. 13:21–5; 14:30; Josh. 2:1.

Lord, have mercy. *Thrice.* Glory . . . Both Now . . .

KONTAKION · TONE 6

My soul, O my soul, rise up! Why art thou sleeping? The end draws near, and soon thou shalt be troubled. Watch, then, that Christ thy God may spare thee, for He is everywhere present and fills all things.

Ode 7

EIRMOS: *We have sinned, we have transgressed, we have done evil in Thy sight; we have not kept or followed Thy commandments. But reject us not utterly, O God of our fathers.*

REFRAIN: *Have mercy on me, O God, have mercy on me.*

When the Ark was being carried in a cart and the ox stumbled, Uzzah did no more than touch it, but the wrath of God smote him. O my soul, flee from his presumption and respect with reverence the things of God.[34]

Thou hast heard of Absalom, and how he rebelled against nature; thou knowest of the unholy deeds by which he defiled his father David's bed. Yet thou hast followed him in his passionate and sensual desires.[35]

Thy free dignity, O my soul, thou hast subjected to thy body; for thou hast found in the enemy another Ahitophel, and hast agreed to all his counsels. But Christ Himself has brought them to nothing and saved thee from them all.[36]

Solomon the wonderful, who was full of the grace of wisdom, once did evil in the sight of heaven and turned away from God. Thou hast become like him, my soul, by thine accursed life.[37]

Carried away by sensual passions, he defiled himself. Alas! The lover of wisdom became a lover of harlots and a stranger to God. And thou, my soul, in mind hast imitated him through thy shameful desires.[38]

O my soul, thou hast rivalled Rehoboam, who paid no attention to his father's counsellors, and Jeroboam, that evil servant and renegade of old. But flee from their example and cry to God: I have sinned, take pity on me.[39]

---

[34] 2 Kgs. [2 Sam.] 6: 6–7.   [35] 2 Kgs. [2 Sam.] 16: 21–2.   [36] 2 Kgs. [2 Sam.] 16: 23.
[37] 3 [1] Kgs. 11: 1–10.   [38] 3 [1] Kgs. 3: 12; 11: 1.   [39] 3 [1] Kgs. 11: 26–40; 12: 1–33.

Glory to the Father, and to the Son, and to the Holy Spirit.

O simple and undivided Trinity, O holy and consubstantial Unity: Thou art praised as Light and Lights, one Holy and three Holies. Sing, O my soul, and glorify Life and Lives, the God of all.

Both now and ever, and unto the ages of ages. Amen.

We praise thee, we bless thee, we venerate thee, O Mother of God: for thou hast given birth to One of the undivided Trinity, thy Son and God, and thou hast opened the heavenly places to us on earth.

Ode 8

EIRMOS: *The hosts of heaven give Him glory; before Him tremble cherubim and seraphim; let everything that has breath and all creation praise Him, bless Him, and exalt Him above all for ever.*

REFRAIN: *Have mercy on me, O God, have mercy on me.*

Thou hast followed Uzziah, my soul, and hast his leprosy in double form: for thy thoughts are wicked, and thine acts unlawful. Leave what thou hast, and hasten to repentance.[40]

O my soul, thou hast heard how the men of Nineveh repented before God in sackcloth and ashes. Yet thou hast not followed them, but art more wicked than all who sinned before the Law and after.[41]

Thou hast heard, my soul, how Jeremiah in the muddy pit cried out with lamentations for the city of Zion and asked to be given tears. Follow his life of lamentation and be saved.[42]

Jonah fled to Tarshish, foreseeing the conversion of the men of Nineveh; for as a prophet he knew the loving-kindness of God, but he was jealous that his prophecy should not be proved false.[43]

My soul, thou hast heard how Daniel stopped the mouths of the wild beasts in the lions' den; and thou knowest how the Children with Azarias quenched through their faith the flames of the fiery furnace.[44]

All the names of the Old Testament have I set before thee, my soul, as an example. Imitate the holy acts of the righteous and flee from the sins of the wicked.

[40]2 Chr. 26: 19.   [41]Jon. 3: 5.   [42]Jer. 45 [38]: 6; 9:1.
[43]Jon. 1: 3..   [44]Dan. 6: 16–22; 3: 23–5.

Glory to the Father, and to the Son, and to the Holy Spirit.

Father without beginning, coeternal Son, and loving Comforter, the Spirit of righteousness; Begetter of the Word of God, Word of the Eternal Father, Spirit living and creative: O Trinity in Unity, have mercy on me.

Both now and ever, and unto the ages of ages. Amen.

As from purple silk, O undefiled Virgin, the spiritual robe of Emmanuel, His flesh, was woven in thy womb. Therefore we honour thee as Theotokos in very truth.

Ode 9

EIRMOS: *Conception without seed; nativity past understanding, from a Mother who never knew a man; childbearing undefiled. For the birth of God makes both natures new. Therefore, as Bride and Mother of God, with true worship all generations magnify thee.*

REFRAIN: *Have mercy on me, O God, have mercy on me.*

Christ was being tempted; the devil tempted Him, showing Him the stones that they might be made bread. He led Him up into a mountain, to see in an instant all the kingdoms of the world. O my soul, look with fear on what happened; watch and pray every hour to God.[45]

The Dove who loved the wilderness, the Lamp of Christ, the voice of one crying aloud, was heard preaching repentance; but Herod sinned with Herodias. O my soul, see that thou art not trapped in the snares of the lawless, but embrace repentance.[46]

The Forerunner of grace went to dwell in the wilderness, and Judaea and all Samaria ran to hear him; they confessed their sins and were baptized eagerly. But thou, my soul, hast not imitated them.[47]

Marriage is honourable, and the marriage-bed undefiled. For on both Christ has given His blessing, eating in the flesh at the wedding in Cana, turning the water into wine and revealing His first miracle, to bring thee, my soul, to a change of life.[48]

[45]Matt. 4: 3–9; 26: 41.   [46]Ps. 54: 7; Jn. 5: 35; Isa. 40: 3; Matt. 3: 2–3; 14: 3; Ps. 123: 7.
[47]Matt. 3: 5–6.   [48]Heb. 13: 4; Jn. 2: 1–11.

Christ gave strength to the paralysed man, and he took up his bed; He raised from the dead the young man, the son of the widow, and the centurion's servant; He appeared to the woman of Samaria and spoke to thee, my soul, of worship in spirit.[49]

By the touch of the hem of His garment, the Lord healed the woman with an issue of blood; He cleansed lepers and gave sight to the blind and made the lame walk upright; He cured by His word the deaf and the dumb and the woman bowed to the ground, to bring thee, wretched soul, to salvation.[50]

Glory to the Father, and to the Son, and to the Holy Spirit.

Let us glorify the Father, let us exalt the Son, and with faith let us worship the Spirit of God, undivided Trinity and Unity in essence. Let us adore Light and Lights, Life and Lives, giving light and life to the ends of the earth.

Both now and ever, and unto the ages of ages. Amen.

Watch over thy City, all-pure Mother of God. For by thee she reigns in faith, by thee she is made strong; by thee she is victorious, putting to flight every temptation, despoiling the enemy and ruling her subjects.

REFRAIN: *Holy father Andrew, pray to God for us.*

Venerable Andrew, father thrice-blessed, shepherd of Crete, cease not to offer prayer for us who sing thy praises; that we may be delivered from all danger and distress, from corruption and sin, who honour thy memory with faith.

AND AGAIN THE EIRMOS: *Conception without seed; nativity past understanding, from a Mother who never knew a man; childbearing undefiled. For the birth of God makes both natures new. Therefore, as Bride and Mother of God, with true worship all generations magnify thee.*

THEN THE REST OF GREAT COMPLINE

[49]Matt. 9: 2–7; Lk. 7: 11–15; Matt. 8: 6–13; Jn. 4: 24.
[50]Matt. 9: 20–22; 11: 5; Lk. 13: 11–13.

Wednesday of the First Week

On Wednesday of the first week of Lent, the Canon is chanted during Great Compline, immediately following Psalm 69. The Eirmoi are sung twice at the beginning of each ode. Only at the Ninth Ode is the Eirmos repeated at the end, in place of "It is truly meet." Before each Troparion we make the sign of the Cross and bow three times.

Ode 1

EIRMOS: *He is for me unto salvation Helper and Protector. He is my God and I glorify Him, God of my fathers is He and I exalt Him, for He is greatly glorified.*

REFRAIN: *Have mercy on me, O God, have mercy on me.*

From my youth, O Saviour, I have rejected Thy commandments. Ruled by the passions, I have passed my whole life in heedlessness and sloth. Therefore I cry to Thee, O Saviour, even now at the end: Save me.

I lie as an outcast before Thy gate, O Saviour. In my old age cast me not down empty into hell; but, before the end comes, in Thy love grant me remission of sins.[1]

As the Prodigal, O Saviour, I have wasted all my substance in riotous living, and I am barren of the virtues of holiness. In my hunger I cry: O compassionate Father, come quickly out to meet me and take pity on me.[2]

I am the man who fell among thieves, even my own thoughts; they have covered all my body with wounds, and I lie beaten and bruised. But come to me, O Christ my Saviour, and heal me.[3]

The Priest saw me first, but passed by on the other side; the Levite looked on me in my distress but despised my nakedness. O Jesus, sprung from Mary, do Thou come to me and take pity on me.[4]

REFRAIN: *Holy mother Mary, pray to God for us.*

Grant me the light of grace, from God's providence on high, that I may flee from the darkness of the passions and sing fervently the joyful tale of thy life, O Mary.

[1] Lk. 16: 20; Ps. 54: 16; 70: 9.   [2] Lk. 15:11–20.   [3] Lk. 10: 30.   [4] Lk. 10: 31–33.

Glory to the Father, and to the Son, and to the Holy Spirit.

Trinity beyond all being, worshipped in Unity, take from me the heavy yoke of sin, and in Thy compassion grant me tears of compunction.

Both now and ever, and unto the ages of ages. Amen.

O Theotokos, the hope and protection of those who sing thy praises, take from me the heavy yoke of sin and, pure Lady, accept me in repentance.

Ode 2

EIRMOS: *Attend, O heaven, and I shall speak and sing in praise of Christ, who took flesh from a Virgin and came to dwell among us.*

REFRAIN: *Have mercy on me, O God, have mercy on me.*

Like David, I have fallen into lust and I am covered with filth; but wash me clean, O Saviour, by my tears.[5]

I have no tears, no repentance, no compunction; but as God do Thou Thyself, O Saviour, bestow them on me.

I have lost the beauty and glory with which I was first created; and now I lie naked and ashamed.

Lord, Lord, at the Last Day shut not Thy door against me; but open it to me, for I repent before Thee.[6]

Give ear to the groaning of my soul, and accept the tears that fall from mine eyes; O Lord, save me.

O Lover of mankind, who desirest that all men shall be saved, in Thy goodness call me back and accept me in repentance.[7]

Most holy Theotokos, save us.

O Theotokos undefiled, Virgin alone worthy of all praise, intercede fervently for our salvation.

ANOTHER EIRMOS: *See now, see that I am God, who rained down manna in the days of old, and made springs of water flow from the rock, for My people in the wilderness, by My right hand and by My power alone.*

REFRAIN: *Have mercy on me, O God, have mercy on me.*

'See now, see that I am God': give ear, my soul, to the Lord as He cries to thee; forsake thy former sin, and fear Him as thy judge and God.

---

[5]2 Kgs. [2 Sam.]11: 2–4.
[6]Matt. 25: 11.   [7]1 Tim. 2: 4.

To whom shall I liken thee, O soul of many sins? Alas! to Cain and to Lamech. For thou hast stoned thy body to death with thine evil deeds, and killed thy mind with thy disordered longings.[8]

Call to mind, my soul, all who lived before the Law. Thou hast not been like Seth, or followed Enos or Enoch, who was translated to heaven, or Noah; but thou art found destitute, without a share in the life of the righteous.[9]

Thou alone, O my soul, hast opened the windows of the wrath of thy God, and thou hast flooded, as the earth, all thy flesh and deeds and life; and thou hast remained outside the Ark of salvation.[10]

REFRAIN: *Holy mother Mary, pray to God for us.*

With all eagerness and love hast thou run to Christ, turning from thy former path of sin, finding thy food in the trackless wilderness, and fulfilling in purity the commandments of God.

Glory to the Father, and to the Son, and to the Holy Spirit.

O Trinity uncreated and without beginning, O undivided Unity: accept me in repentance and save me, a sinner. I am Thy creation, reject me not; but spare me and deliver me from the fire of condemnation.

Both now and ever, and unto the ages of ages. Amen.

Most pure Lady, Mother of God, the hope of those who run to thee and the haven of the storm-tossed: pray to the merciful God, thy Creator and thy Son, that He may grant His mercy even to me.

Ode 3

EIRMOS: *O Lord, upon the rock of Thy commandments make firm my wavering heart, for Thou alone art Holy and Lord.*

REFRAIN: *Have mercy on me, O God, have mercy on me.*

O wretched soul, thou hast not inherited the blessing of Shem, nor hast thou received, like Japhet, a spacious domain in the land of forgiveness.[11]

O my soul, depart from sin, from the land of Haran, and come to the land that Abraham inherited, which flows with incorruption and eternal life.[12]

Thou hast heard, my soul, how Abraham in days of old left the land of his fathers and became a wanderer: follow him in his choice.[13]

---

[8]Gen. 4: 8, 23..   [9]Gen. 5, 3, 6: 21–4; 6: 9.   [10]Gen. 7: 11–13.
[11]Gen. 9: 26–27.   [12]Gen. 11:31–12:1; Ex. 3:8.   [13]Gen. 12: 1.

At the oak of Mamre the Patriarch gave hospitality to the angels, and in his old age he inherited the reward of the promise.[14]

Thou knowest, O my miserable soul, how Isaac was offered mystically as a new and unwonted sacrifice to the Lord: follow him in his choice.[15]

Thou hast heard—O my soul be watchful! —how Ishmael was driven out as the child of a bondwoman. Take heed, lest the same thing happen to thee because of thy lust.[16]

REFRAIN: *Holy mother Mary, pray to God for us.*

I am held fast, O Mother, by the tempest and billows of sin: but do thou keep me safe and lead me to the haven of divine repentance.

REFRAIN: *Holy mother Mary, pray to God for us.*

O holy Mary, offer thy prayer of supplication to the compassionate Theotokos, and through thine intercessions open unto me the door that leads to God.

Glory to the Father, and to the Son, and to the Holy Spirit.

O simple Unity praised in Trinity of Persons, uncreated Nature without beginning, save us who in faith worship Thy power.

Both now and ever, and unto the ages of ages. Amen.

O Mother of God, without knowing man thou hast given birth within time to the Son, who was begotten outside time from the Father; and, strange wonder! thou givest suck while still remaining Virgin.

Ode 4

EIRMOS: *The Prophet heard of Thy coming, O Lord, and he was afraid: how Thou wast to be born of a Virgin and revealed to men, and he said: 'I have heard the report of Thee and I was afraid.' Glory to Thy power, O Lord.*

REFRAIN: *Have mercy on me, O God, have mercy on me.*

I have defiled my body, I have stained my spirit, and I am all covered with wounds: but as physician, Christ, heal both body and spirit for me through repentance. Wash, purify and cleanse me, O my Saviour, and make me whiter than snow.

---

[14]Gen. 18: 1–15.   [15]Gen. 22: 1–14.   [16]Gen. 21: 10.

Thy Body and Thy Blood, O Word, Thou hast offered at Thy Crucifixion for the sake of all: Thy Body to refashion me, Thy Blood to wash me clean; and Thou hast given up Thy spirit, O Christ, to bring me to Thy Father.

O compassionate Lord, Thou hast worked salvation in the midst of the earth, that we might be saved. Thou wast crucified of Thine own will upon the Tree; and Eden, closed till then, was opened. Things above and things below, the creation and all the peoples have been saved and worship Thee.[17]

May the Blood from Thy side be to me a cleansing fount, and may the water that flows with it be a drink of forgiveness. May I be purified by both, O Word, anointed and refreshed, having as chrism and drink Thy words of life.[18]

As a chalice, O my Saviour, the Church has been granted Thy life-giving side, from which there flows down to us a twofold stream of forgiveness and knowledge, representing the two covenants, the Old and the New.[19]

I am deprived of the bridal chamber, of the wedding and the supper; for want of oil my lamp has gone out; while I slept the door was closed; the supper has been eaten; I am bound hand and foot, and cast out.[20]

Glory to the Father, and to the Son, and to the Holy Spirit.

Undivided in Essence, unconfused in Persons, I confess Thee as God: Triune Deity, one in kingship and throne; and to Thee I raise the great thrice-holy hymn that is sung on high.[21]

Both now and ever, and unto the ages of ages. Amen.

Thou givest birth and art a virgin, and in both thou remainest by nature inviolate. He who is born makes new the laws of nature, and the womb brings forth without travail. When God so wills, the natural order is overcome; for He does whatever He wishes.

Ode 5

EIRMOS: *From the night I seek Thee early, O Lover of mankind: give me light, I pray Thee, and guide me in Thy commandments, and teach me, O Saviour, to do Thy will.*

REFRAIN: *Have mercy on me, O God, have mercy on me.*

---

[17]Ps. 73:12.   [18]Jn. 19: 34; 6:55.   [19]Exod. 24: 8; Matt. 26: 28; Jn. 19: 34.
[20]Matt. 25: 1–13; 22:11–13.   [21]Isa. 6: 3; Rev. 4: 8..

In my soul and body, O Lord, I have become like Jannes and Jambres, the magicians of cruel Pharaoh; my will is heavy and my mind is drowned beneath the waters. But do Thou come to my aid.[22]

Woe is me! I have defiled my mind with filth. But I pray to Thee, O Master: wash me clean in the waters of my tears, and make the garment of my flesh white as snow.

When I examine my actions, O Saviour, I see that I have gone beyond all men in sin; for I knew and understood what I did; I was not sinning in ignorance.

Spare, O spare the work of Thine hands, O Lord. I have sinned, forgive me: for Thou alone art pure by nature, and none save Thee is free from defilement.

Thou who art God, O Saviour, wast for my sake fashioned as I am. Thou hast performed miracles, healing lepers, giving strength to the paralysed, stopping the issue of blood when the woman touched the hem of Thy garment.[23]

REFRAIN: *Holy mother Mary, pray to God for us.*

Crossing the stream of Jordan, thou hast found peace, escaping from the deadening pleasures of the flesh. Deliver us also from them, holy Mary, by thine intercessions.

Glory to the Father, and to the Son, and to the Holy Spirit.

We glorify Thee, O Trinity, the one God. Holy, holy, holy, art Thou: Father, Son and Spirit, simple Essence and Unity, worshipped for ever.

Both now and ever, and unto the ages of ages. Amen.

O Virgin inviolate and Mother who hast not known man, from thee has God, the Creator of the ages, taken human flesh, uniting to Himself the nature of men.

Ode 6

EIRMOS: *With my whole heart I cried to the all-compassionate God: and He heard me from the lowest depths of hell, and brought my life out of corruption.*

REFRAIN: *Have mercy on me, O God, have mercy on me.*

---

[22]Exod. 7: 11; 2 Tim. 3: 8.   [23]Phil. 2:6–7; Matt. 4: 24; Lk. 17:12–14; 5:18; 8: 43–48.

Rise up and make war upon the passions of the flesh, as Joshua against Amalek, ever gaining the victory over the Gibeonites, thy deceitful thoughts.[24]

O my soul, pass through the flowing waters of time like the Ark of old, and take possession of the land of promise: for God commands thee.[25]

As Thou hast saved Peter when he cried out, 'Save me', come quickly, O Saviour, before it is too late, and save me from the beast. Stretch out Thine hand and lead me up from the deep of sin.[26]

I know Thee as a calm haven, O Lord, Lord Christ: come quickly, before it is too late, and deliver me from the lowest depths of sin and despair.

Glory to the Father, and to the Son, and to the Holy Spirit.

'I am the Trinity, simple and undivided, yet divided in Persons, and I am the Unity, by Nature one', says the Father and the Son and the divine Spirit.

Both now and ever, and unto the ages of ages. Amen.

Thy womb bore God for us, fashioned in our shape. O Theotokos, pray to Him as the Creator of all, that we may be justified through thine intercessions.

Lord, have mercy. *Thrice.* Glory . . . Both Now . . .

KONTAKION · TONE 6

My soul, O my soul, rise up! Why art thou sleeping? The end draws near, and soon thou shalt be troubled. Watch, then, that Christ our God may spare thee, for He is everywhere present and fills all things.

Ode 7

EIRMOS: *We have sinned, we have transgressed, we have done evil in Thy sight; we have not kept or followed Thy commandments. But reject us not utterly, O God of our fathers.*

REFRAIN: *Have mercy on me, O God, have mercy on me.*

By deliberate choice, my soul, thou hast incurred the guilt of Manasseh, setting up the passions as idols and multiplying abominations. But with fervent heart emulate his repentance and acquire compunction.[27]

---

[24]Ex.17: 8–13; Josh. 9: 3–27.   [25]Josh. 3:15–7; Deut. 1: 8.

[26]Matt. 14: 30–31; Dan. 7:11; Rev. 13;1.

[27]4 [2] Kgs. 21:1–16; 2 Chron. 33:11–13; the Prayer of Manasseh.

Alas, my soul! Thou hast rivalled Ahab in guilt. Thou hast become a dwelling-place of fleshly defilements and a shameful vessel of the passions. But groan from the depths of thy heart, and confess thy sins to God.[28]

Heaven is closed to thee, my soul, and a famine from God has seized thee: for thou hast been disobedient, as Ahab was to the words of Elijah the Tishbite. But imitate the widow of Zarephath, and feed the prophet's soul.[29]

Elijah once destroyed with fire twice fifty of Jezebel's servants, and he slew the prophets of shame, as a rebuke to Ahab. But flee from the example of both of them, my soul, and be strong.[30]

Glory to the Father, and to the Son, and to the Holy Spirit.

O simple and undivided Trinity, O holy and consubstantial Unity: Thou art praised as Light and Lights, one Holy and three Holies. Sing, O my soul, and glorify Life and Lives, the God of all.

Both now and ever, and unto the ages of ages. Amen.

We praise thee, we bless thee, we venerate thee, O Mother of God: for thou hast given birth to One of the undivided Trinity, thy Son and God, and thou hast opened the heavenly places to us on earth.

Ode 8

EIRMOS: *The hosts of heaven give Him glory; before Him tremble cherubim and seraphim; let everything that has breath and all creation praise Him, bless Him, and exalt Him above all for ever.*

REFRAIN: *Have mercy on me, O God, have mercy on me.*

O righteous Judge and Saviour, have mercy on me and deliver me from the fire that threatens me and from the punishment that I deserve to suffer at the Judgement. Before the end comes, grant me remission through virtue and repentance.

Like the Thief I cry to Thee, 'Remember me'; like Peter I weep bitterly; like the Publican I call out, 'Forgive me, Saviour'; like the Harlot I shed tears. Accept my lamentation, as once Thou hast accepted the entreaties of the woman of Canaan.[31]

---

[28]3 [1] Kgs. 16: 30.   [29]3 [1] Kgs. 17:1,9; Luke 4:25.
[30]4 [2] Kgs. 1: 10–15; 3 [1] Kgs. 18: 40.
[31]Lk. 23: 42; Matt. 26: 75; Lk. 18: 13; 7: 37–38; Matt. 15: 22–28.

O Saviour, heal the putrefaction of my humbled soul, for Thou art the one Physician; apply plaster and pour in oil and wine—works of repentance, and compunction with tears.[32]

Like the woman of Canaan I cry to Thee, 'Have mercy on me, Son of David.' Like the woman with an issue of blood, I touch the hem of Thy garment. I weep as Martha and Mary wept for Lazarus.[33]

Glory to the Father, and to the Son, and to the Holy Spirit.

Father without beginning, coeternal Son, and loving Comforter, the Spirit of righteousness; Begetter of the Word of God, Word of the Eternal Father, Spirit living and creative: O Trinity in Unity, have mercy on me.

Both now and ever, and unto the ages of ages. Amen.

As from purple silk, O undefiled Virgin, the spiritual robe of Emmanuel, His flesh, was woven in thy womb. Therefore we honour thee as Theotokos in very truth.

Ode 9

EIRMOS: *Conception without seed; nativity past understanding, from a Mother who never knew a man; childbearing undefiled. For the birth of God makes both natures new. Therefore, as Bride and Mother of God, with true worship all generations magnify thee.*

REFRAIN: *Have mercy on me, O God, have mercy on me.*

Healing sickness, Christ the Word preached the good tidings to the poor. He cured the crippled, ate with publicans, and conversed with sinners. With the touch of His hand, He brought back the departed soul of Jairus' daughter.[34]

The Publican was saved and the Harlot turned to chastity, but the Pharisee with his boasting was condemned. For the first cried 'Be merciful', and the second, 'Have mercy on me'; but the third said, boasting, 'I thank Thee, O God', and other words of madness.[35]

Zacchaeus was a publican, yet he was saved; but Simon the Pharisee went astray, while the Harlot received remission and release from Him who has the power to forgive sins. Make haste, O my soul, to follow her example.[36]

---

[32]Lk. 10: 34.   [33]Matt. 15: 22; Lk. 8:43–44; Jn. 11: 33.
[34]Lk 4:17–19; 5:27–30; Matt. 11:5; Mk. 5: 41–42.
[35]Lk. 7: 36–50; 18: 9–13.   [36]Lk. 19: 1–10; 7: 36–50.

O wretched soul, thou hast not acted like the Harlot, who took the alabaster box of precious ointment, and anointed with tears and wiped with her hair the feet of the Lord. And He tore in pieces the record of her previous sins.[37]

Thou knowest, O my soul, how the cities were cursed to which Christ preached the Gospel. Fear their example, lest thou suffer the same punishment. For the Master likened them to Sodom and condemned them to hell.[38]

Be not overcome by despair, my soul; for thou hast heard of the faith of the woman of Canaan, and how through it her daughter was healed by the word of God. Cry out from the depth of thy heart, 'Save me also, Son of David', as she once cried to Christ.[39]

Glory to the Father, and to the Son, and to the Holy Spirit.

Let us glorify the Father, let us exalt the Son, and with faith let us worship the Spirit of God, undivided Trinity and Unity in essence. Let us adore Light and Lights, Life and Lives, giving light and life to the ends of the earth.

Both now and ever, and unto the ages of ages. Amen.

Watch over thy City, all-pure Mother of God. For by thee she reigns in faith, by thee she is made strong; by thee she is victorious, putting to flight every temptation, despoiling the enemy and ruling her subjects.

REFRAIN: *Holy father Andrew, pray to God for us.*

Venerable Andrew, father thrice-blessed, shepherd of Crete, cease not to offer prayer for us who sing thy praises; that we may be delivered from all danger and distress, from corruption and sin, who honour thy memory with faith.

AND AGAIN THE EIRMOS: *Conception without seed; nativity past understanding, from a Mother who never knew a man; childbearing undefiled. For the birth of God makes both natures new. Therefore, as Bride and Mother of God, with true worship all generations magnify thee.*

THEN THE REST OF GREAT COMPLINE

[37]Lk. 7: 37–38; Col. 2: 14.
[38]Lk. 10: 13–15.
[39]Matt. 15: 22.

Thursday of the First Week

On Thursday of the first week of Lent, the Canon is chanted during Great Compline, immediately following Psalm 69. The Eirmoi are sung twice at the beginning of each ode. Only at the Ninth Ode is the Eirmos repeated at the end, in place of "It is truly meet." Before each Troparion we make the sign of the Cross and bow three times.

Ode 1 · Tone 6

EIRMOS: *He is for me unto salvation Helper and Protector. He is my God and I glorify Him, God of my fathers is He and I exalt Him, for He is greatly glorified.*

REFRAIN: *Have mercy on me, O God, have mercy on me.*

O Lamb of God, that takest away the sins of all, take from me the heavy yoke of sin, and in Thy compassion give me tears of compunction.[1]

I fall down, Jesus, at Thy feet: I have sinned against Thee, be merciful to me. Take from me the heavy yoke of sin, and in Thy compassion, O God, accept me in repentance.

Enter not into judgement with me, bringing before me the things I should have done, examining my words and correcting my impulses. But in Thy mercy overlook my sins and save me, O Lord almighty.[2]

It is time for repentance: to Thee I come, my Creator. Take from me the heavy yoke of sin, and in Thy compassion give me tears of compunction.

As the Prodigal, O Saviour, I have wasted the substance of my soul in sin, and I am barren of the virtues of holiness. In my hunger I cry: O Giver of mercy, come quickly out to meet me and take pity on me.[3]

REFRAIN: *Holy mother Mary, pray to God for us.*

Bowing before the divine laws of Christ, thou hast drawn near to Him, forsaking the unbridled longings of sensual pleasure; and in the fear of God thou hast gained all the virtues as if they were one.

Glory to the Father, and to the Son, and to the Holy Spirit.

[1] Jn. 1: 29. [2] Ps. 142: 2. [3] Lk. 15: 11–20.

Trinity beyond all being, worshipped in Unity, take from me the heavy yoke of sin, and in Thy compassion grant me tears of compunction.

Both now and ever, and unto the ages of ages. Amen.

O Theotokos, the hope and protection of those who sing thy praises, take from me the heavy yoke of sin and, pure Lady, accept me in repentance.

Ode 2

EIRMOS: *See now, see that I am God, who rained down manna in the days of old, and made springs of water flow from the rock, for My people in the wilderness, by My right hand and by My power alone.*

REFRAIN: *Have mercy on me, O God, have mercy on me.*

'I have slain a man to my grief and wounding', said Lamech, 'and a young man to my hurt'; and he cried aloud lamenting. Dost thou not tremble then, my soul, for thou hast defiled thy flesh and polluted thy mind?[4]

Skilfully hast thou planned to build a tower, O my soul, and to establish a stronghold for thy lusts; but the Creator confounded thy designs and dashed thy devices to the ground.[5]

Ah, how I have emulated Lamech, the murderer of old, slaying my soul as if it were a man, and my mind as if it were a young man. With sensual longings I have killed my body, as Cain the murderer killed his brother.[6]

Roused to anger by their transgressions, the Lord once rained down fire from heaven and burnt up the men of Sodom. And thou, my soul, hast kindled the fire of Gehenna, and there to thy bitter sorrow thou shalt burn.[7]

I am wounded and smitten: see the enemy's arrows which have pierced my soul and body. See the wounds, the open sores and the injuries, that cry out to God against the blows inflicted by my freely-chosen passions.

REFRAIN: *Holy mother Mary, pray to God for us.*

Sunk in the abyss of wickedness, O Mary, thou hast lifted up thine hands to the merciful God. And, as to Peter, in His loving-kindness He stretched out His hand to thee in help, seeking in every way thy conversion.[8]

Glory to the Father, and to the Son, and to the Holy Spirit.

---

[4]Gen. 4: 23.   [5]Gen. 11: 3–8.   [6]Gen. 4: 23, 4: 6–8.
[7]Gen. 19: 24.; Matt 5:22.   [8]Matt. 14: 31.

O Trinity uncreated and without beginning, O undivided Unity, accept me in repentance and save me, a sinner. I am Thy creation, reject me not; but spare me and deliver me from the fire of condemnation.

Both now and ever, and unto the ages of ages. Amen.

Most pure Lady, Mother of God, the hope of those who run to thee and the haven of the storm-tossed: pray to the merciful God, thy Creator and thy Son, that He may grant His mercy even to me.

Ode 3

EIRMOS: *O Lord, upon the rock of Thy commandments make firm my wavering heart, for Thou alone art Holy and Lord.*

REFRAIN: *Have mercy on me, O God, have mercy on me.*

O my soul, thou hast become like Hagar the Egyptian: thy free choice has been enslaved, and thou hast borne as thy child a new Ishmael, stubborn wilfulness.[9]

Thou knowest, my soul, the ladder that was shown to Jacob, reaching up from earth to heaven. Why hast thou not provided a firm foundation for it through thy godly actions?[10]

Follow the example of Melchizedek, the priest of God, the King set apart, who was an image of the life of Christ among men in the world.[11]

Turn back, wretched soul, and lament, before the fair-ground of life comes to an end, before the Lord shuts the door of the bridal chamber.[12]

Do not look back, my soul, and so be turned into a pillar of salt. Fear the example of the people of Sodom, and take refuge in Zoar.[13]

Reject not, O Master, the prayer of those who sing Thy praises, but in Thy loving-kindness be merciful and grant forgiveness to them that ask with faith.

Glory to the Father, and to the Son, and to the Holy Spirit.

O simple Unity praised in Trinity of Persons, uncreated Nature without beginning, save us who in faith worship Thy power.

Both now and ever, and unto the ages of ages. Amen.

---

[9]Gen. 16: 3, 15.   [10]Gen. 28: 12.   [11]Gen. 14: 18: Heb. 7: 1–3.
[12]Matt. 25:10.   [13]Gen. 19: 23, 26.

O Mother of God, without knowing man thou hast given birth within time to the Son, who was begotten outside time from the Father; and, strange wonder! thou givest suck while still remaining Virgin.

Ode 4

EIRMOS: *The prophet heard of Thy coming, O Lord, and he was afraid: how Thou wast to be born of a Virgin and revealed to men, and he said: 'I have heard the report of Thee and I was afraid.' Glory to Thy power, O Lord.*

REFRAIN: *Have mercy on me, O God, have mercy on me.*

The time of my life is short, filled with trouble and evil. But accept me in repentance and call me back to knowledge. Let me not become the possession and food of the enemy; but do Thou, O Saviour, take pity on me.

A man of great wealth and righteous, abounding in riches and cattle, clothed in royal dignity, in crown and purple robe, Job became suddenly a beggar, stripped of wealth, glory and kingship.[14]

If he who was righteous and blameless above all men did not escape the snares and pits of the deceiver, what wilt thou do, wretched and sin-loving soul, when some sudden misfortune befalls thee?[15]

Now I speak boastfully, with boldness of heart; yet all to no purpose and in vain. O righteous Judge, who alone art compassionate, do not condemn me with the Pharisee; but grant me the abasement of the Publican and number me with him.[16]

I know, O compassionate Lord, that I have sinned and violated the vessel of my flesh. But accept me in repentance and call me back to knowledge. Let me not become the possession and food of the enemy; but do Thou, O Saviour, take pity on me.

I have become mine own idol, utterly defiling my soul with the passions. But accept me in repentance and call me back to knowledge. Let me not become the possession and food of the enemy; but do Thou, O Saviour, take pity on me.

I have not hearkened to Thy voice, I have not heeded Thy Scripture, O Giver of the Law. But accept me in repentance and call me back to knowledge. Let me not become the possession and food of the enemy; but do Thou, O Saviour, take pity on me.

---

[14]Job 1: 1–22.   [15]Job 2: 3–6.   [16]Lk. 18: 9–14.

REFRAIN: *Holy mother Mary, pray to God for us.*

Thou wast brought down into an abyss of great iniquity, yet not held fast within it: but with better intent thou hast mounted through action to the height of virtue, past all expectation: and the angels, O Mary, were amazed at thee.

Glory to the Father, and to the Son, and to the Holy Spirit.

Undivided in Essence, unconfused in Persons, I confess Thee as God: Triune Deity, one in kingship and throne; and to Thee I raise the great thrice-holy hymn that is sung on high.[17]

Both now and ever, and unto the ages of ages. Amen.

Thou givest birth and art a virgin, and in both thou remainest by nature inviolate. He who is born makes new the laws of nature, and the womb brings forth without travail. When God so wills, the natural order is overcome: for He does whatever He wishes.

Ode 5

EIRMOS: *From the night I seek Thee early, O Lover of mankind: give me light, I pray Thee, and guide me in Thy commandments, and teach me, O Saviour, to do Thy will.*

REFRAIN: *Have mercy on me, O God, have mercy on me.*

O my soul, do as the woman who was bowed down to the ground. Fall at the feet of Jesus, that He may make thee straight again; and thou shalt walk upright upon the paths of the Lord.[18]

Thou art a deep well, O Master: make springs gush forth for me from Thy pure veins, that like the woman of Samaria I may drink and thirst no more; for from Thee flow the streams of life.[19]

O Master and Lord, may my tears be unto me as Siloam: that I also may wash clean the eyes of my heart, and with my mind behold Thee, the pre-eternal Light.[20]

REFRAIN: *Holy mother Mary, pray to God for us.*

O blessed saint, with a love beyond compare thou hast longed to venerate the Wood of the Cross, and thy desire was granted. Make me also worthy to attain the glory on high.

---

[17]Isa. 6:3; Rev. 4:8.   [18]Lk. 13: 11–13.   [19]Jn. 4: 13–15.   [20]Jn. 9: 7.

Glory to the Father, and to the Son, and to the Holy Spirit.

We glorify Thee, O Trinity, the one God. Holy, holy, holy, art Thou, Father, Son and Spirit, simple Essence and Unity, worshipped for ever.

Both now and ever, and unto the ages of ages. Amen.

O Virgin inviolate and Mother who hast not known man, from thee has God, the Creator of the ages, taken human flesh, uniting to Himself the nature of men.

Ode 6

EIRMOS: *With my whole heart I cried to the all-compassionate God: and He heard me from the lowest depths of hell, and brought my life out of corruption.*

REFRAIN: *Have mercy on me, O God, have mercy on me.*

O Saviour, I am the coin marked with the King's likeness, which Thou hast lost of old. But, O Word, light Thy lamp, Thy Forerunner, and seek and find again Thine image.[21]

Rise up and make war upon the passions of the flesh, as Joshua against Amalek, ever gaining the victory over the Gibeonites, thy deceitful thoughts.[22]

REFRAIN: *Holy mother Mary, pray to God for us.*

Thy soul on fire, O Mary, thou hast ever shed streams of tears, to quench the burning of the passions. Grant the grace of these thy tears to me also, thy servant.

REFRAIN: *Holy mother Mary, pray to God for us.*

Through the perfection of thine earthly life, O Mother, thou hast gained a heavenly freedom from the sinfulness of passion. In thine intercessions pray that this same freedom may be given to those who sing thy praises.

Glory to the Father, and to the Son, and to the Holy Spirit.

'I am the Trinity, simple and undivided, yet divided in Persons, and I am the Unity, by Nature one', says the Father and the Son and the divine Spirit.

Both now and ever, and unto the ages of ages. Amen.

Thy womb bore God for us, fashioned in our shape. O Theotokos, pray to Him as the Creator of all, that we may be justified through thine intercessions.

---

[21]Lk. 15: 8; Jn 5:35.   [22]Ex.17: 8–13; Josh. 9:3–27.

Lord, have mercy. *Thrice.* Glory . . . Both Now . . .

KONTAKION · TONE 6

My soul, O my soul, rise up! Why art thou sleeping? The end draws near, and soon thou shalt be troubled. Watch, then, that Christ our God may spare thee, for He is everywhere present and fills all things.

Ode 7

EIRMOS: *We have sinned, we have transgressed, we have done evil in Thy sight; we have not kept or followed Thy commandments. But reject us not utterly, O God of our fathers.*

REFRAIN: *Have mercy on me, O God, have mercy on me.*

My days have vanished as a dream of one awaking; and so, like Hezekiah, I weep upon my bed, that years may be added to my life. But what Isaiah will come to me, O my soul, except the God of all?[23]

I fall before Thee, and as tears I offer Thee my words. I have sinned as the Harlot never sinned, and I have transgressed as no other man on earth. But take pity on Thy creature, O Master, and call me back.[24]

I have discoloured Thine image and broken Thy commandment. All my beauty is destroyed and my lamp is quenched by the passions, O Saviour. But take pity on me, as David sings, and 'restore to me Thy joy.'[25]

Turn back, repent, uncover all that thou hast hidden. Say unto God, to whom all things are known: Thou alone knowest my secrets, O Saviour; 'have mercy on me', as David sings, 'according to Thy mercy.'[26]

REFRAIN: *Holy mother Mary, pray to God for us.*

Raising thy cry to the pure Mother of God, thou hast driven back the fury of the passions that violently assailed thee, and put to shame the enemy who sought to make thee stumble. But give thy help in trouble now to me also, thy servant.

REFRAIN: *Holy mother Mary, pray to God for us.*

Pray to Him whom thou hast loved, O holy Mary, whom thou hast desired, for whose sake thou hast worn out thy flesh: pray to Christ for us thy servants, that He may show mercy to us all, and grant a peaceful life to those who worship Him.

[23]Ps. 72:20; 4 [2] Kgs. 20:1–6; Is. 38 :1–8.   [24]Lk. 7: 37.   [25]Ps. 50: 14.   [26]Ps. 50:3.

Glory to the Father, and to the Son, and to the Holy Spirit.

O simple and undivided Trinity, O holy and consubstantial Unity: Thou art praised as Light and Lights, one Holy and three Holies. Sing, O my soul, and glorify Life and Lives, the God of all.

Both now and ever, and unto the ages of ages. Amen.

We praise thee, we bless thee, we venerate thee, O Mother of God: for thou hast given birth to One of the undivided Trinity, thy Son and God, and thou hast opened the heavenly places to us on earth.

Ode 8

EIRMOS: *The hosts of heaven give Him glory; before Him tremble cherubim and seraphim; let everything that has breath and all creation praise Him, bless Him, and exalt Him above all for ever.*

REFRAIN: *Have mercy on me, O God, have mercy on me.*

As precious ointment, O Saviour, I empty on Thine head the alabaster box of my tears. Like the Harlot, I cry out to Thee, seeking Thy mercy: I bring my prayer and ask to receive forgiveness.[27]

No one has sinned against Thee as I have; yet accept even me, compassionate Saviour, for I repent in fear and cry with longing: Against Thee alone have I sinned; I have transgressed, have mercy on me.[28]

Spare the work of Thine own hands, O Saviour, and as shepherd seek the lost sheep that has gone astray. Snatch me from the wolf and make me a nursling in the pasture of Thine own flock.[29]

When Thou sittest upon Thy throne, O merciful Judge, and revealest Thy dread glory, O Christ, what fear there will be then! When the furnace burns with fire, and all shrink back in terror before Thy judgement-seat.[30]

REFRAIN: *Holy mother Mary, pray to God for us.*

The Mother of the Light that never sets illumined thee and freed thee from the darkness of the passions. O Mary, who hast received the grace of the Spirit, give light to those who praise thee with faith.

REFRAIN: *Holy mother Mary, pray to God for us.*

---

[27]Matt. 26: 7; Lk. 7: 37–38.   [28]Ps.50: 6.
[29]Ps. 118: 176; Lk. 15:4; Jn. 10:11–12.
[30]Dan. 7:9–10; Jn. 5:22; Matt. 24:30.

The holy Zosimas was struck with amazement, O Mother, beholding in thee a wonder truly strange and new. For he saw an angel in the body and was filled with astonishment, praising Christ unto all ages.

Glory to the Father, and to the Son, and to the Holy Spirit.

Father without beginning, coeternal Son, and loving Comforter, the Spirit of righteousness; Begetter of the Word of God, Word of the Eternal Father, Spirit living and creative: O Trinity in Unity, have mercy on me.

Both now and ever, and unto the ages of ages. Amen.

As from purple silk, O undefiled Virgin, the spiritual robe of Emmanuel, His flesh, was woven in thy womb. Therefore we honour thee as Theotokos in very truth.

Ode 9

EIRMOS: *Conception without seed; nativity past understanding, from a Mother who never knew a man; childbearing undefiled. For the birth of God makes both natures new. Therefore, as Bride and Mother of God, with true worship all generations magnify thee.*

REFRAIN: *Have mercy on me, O God, have mercy on me.*

O Son of David, with Thy word Thou hast healed the possessed: take pity on me, save me and have mercy. Let me hear Thy compassionate voice speak to me as to the thief: 'Verily, I say unto thee, thou shalt be with Me in Paradise, when I come in My glory.'[31]

A thief accused Thee, a thief confessed Thy Godhead: for both were hanging beside Thee on the Cross. Open to me also, O Lord of many mercies, the door of Thy glorious Kingdom, as once it was opened to Thy thief who acknowledged Thee with faith as God.[32]

The creation was in anguish, seeing Thee crucified. Mountains and rocks were split from fear, the earth quaked, and hell was despoiled; the light grew dark in daytime, beholding Thee, O Jesus, nailed in the flesh.[33]

Do not demand from me worthy fruits of repentance, for my strength has failed within me. Give me an ever-contrite heart and poverty of spirit, that I may offer these to Thee as an acceptable sacrifice, O only Saviour.[34]

---

[31]Matt. 15:22–28; Lk. 9: 38–42; 23: 43.   [32]Lk. 23: 32, 39–43.
[33]Matt. 27: 51–53; Lk. 23: 44 – 45.   [34]Matt. 3: 8; 5: 3; Ps. 50: 19.

O my Judge who dost know me, when Thou comest again with the angels to judge the whole world, look upon me then with Thine eye of mercy and spare me; take pity on me, Jesus, for I have sinned more than any other man.

REFRAIN: *Holy mother Mary, pray to God for us.*

By thy strange way of life thou hast struck all with wonder, both the hosts of angels and the gatherings of mortal men; for thou hast surpassed nature and lived as though no longer in the body. Like a bodiless angel thou hast walked upon the Jordan with thy feet, O Mary, and crossed over it.

REFRAIN: *Holy mother Mary, pray to God for us.*

O holy Mother, call down the gracious mercy of the Creator upon us who sing thy praises, that we may be set free from the sufferings and afflictions that assail us; so without ceasing, delivered from temptations, we shall magnify the Lord who has glorified thee.

REFRAIN: *Holy father Andrew, pray to God for us.*

Venerable Andrew, father thrice-blessed, shepherd of Crete, cease not to offer prayer for us who sing thy praises; that we may be delivered from all danger and distress, from corruption and sin, who honour thy memory with faith.

Glory to the Father, and to the Son, and to the Holy Spirit.

Let us glorify the Father, let us exalt the Son, and with faith let us worship the Spirit of God, undivided Trinity and Unity in essence. Let us adore Light and Lights, Life and Lives, giving light and life to the ends of the earth.

Both now and ever, and unto the ages of ages. Amen.

Watch over thy City, all-pure Mother of God. For by thee she reigns in faith, by thee she is made strong; by thee she is victorious, putting to flight every temptation, despoiling the enemy and ruling her subjects.

AND AGAIN THE EIRMOS: *Conception without seed; nativity past understanding, from a Mother who never knew a man; childbearing undefiled. For the birth of God makes both natures new. Therefore, as Bride and Mother of God, with true worship all generations magnify thee.*

THEN THE REST OF GREAT COMPLINE

Triodion

Thursday of the Fifth Week of Lent

The Order of the Great Canon of Saint Andrew of Crete

We serve Matins for the fifth Thursday of Great Lent on Wednesday evening, beginning in the usual lenten fashion. The first half of the Life of Saint Mary of Egypt is read after the 8th Kathisma and its accompanying sedalia (sessional hymns) from the Triodion. After Psalm 50, we begin to chant the Canon, slowly and with compunction. Before each Troparion we make the sign of the Cross and bow three times.

The Great Canon

THE WORK OF SAINT ANDREW OF CRETE

Ode 1 · Tone 6

EIRMOS: *He is for me unto salvation Helper and Protector. He is my God and I glorify Him, God of my fathers is He and I exalt Him, for He is greatly glorified.*

REFRAIN: *Have mercy on me, O God, have mercy on me.*

Where shall I begin to weep for the actions of my wretched life? What first-fruit shall I offer, O Christ, in this my lamentation? But in Thy compassion grant me forgiveness of sins.

Come, wretched soul, with thy flesh to the Creator of all. Make confession to Him, and abstain henceforth from thy past brutishness; and offer to God tears of repentance.

I have rivalled in transgression Adam the first-formed man, and I have found myself stripped naked of God, of the eternal Kingdom and its joy, because of my sins.[1]

---

[1]Gen. 3: 7–11.

Woe to thee, miserable soul! How like thou art to the first Eve! For thou hast looked in wickedness and wast grievously wounded; thou hast touched the tree and rashly tasted the deceptive food.[2]

Instead of the visible Eve, I have the Eve of the mind: the passionate thought in my flesh, shewing me what seems sweet; yet whenever I taste from it, I find it bitter.

Adam was justly banished from Eden because he disobeyed one commandment of Thine, O Saviour. What then shall I suffer, for I am always rejecting Thy words of life?

By my own free choice I have incurred the guilt of Cain's murder. I have killed my conscience, bringing the flesh to life and making war upon the soul by my wicked actions.[3]

O Jesus, I have not been like Abel in his righteousness. Never have I offered Thee acceptable gifts or godly actions, a pure sacrifice or a life unblemished.[4]

Like Cain, O miserable soul, we too have offered, to the Creator of all, defiled actions and a polluted sacrifice and a worthless life; and so we also are condemned.[5]

As the potter moulds the clay, Thou hast fashioned me, giving me flesh and bones, breath and life. But accept me in repentance, O my Maker and Deliverer and Judge.[6]

I confess to Thee, O Saviour, the sins I have committed, the wounds of my soul and body, which murderous thoughts, like thieves, have inflicted inwardly upon me.[7]

Though I have sinned, O Saviour, yet I know that Thou art full of loving-kindness. Thou dost chastise with mercy and art fervent in compassion. Thou dost see me weeping and dost run to meet me, like the Father calling back the Prodigal Son.[8]

I lie as an outcast before Thy gate, O Saviour. In my old age cast me not down empty into hell; but, before the end comes, in Thy love grant me remission of sins.[9]

I am the man who fell among thieves, even my own thoughts; they have covered all my body with wounds, and I lie beaten and bruised. But come to me, O Christ my Saviour, and heal me.[10]

[2]Gen. 3: 23; Acts 7:38.   [3]Gen. 4: 8.   [4]Gen. 4: 4.
[5]Gen. 4: 5; Heb. 11: 4.   [6]Gen. 2: 7; Jer. 18: 1–10; Rom. 9: 21.
[7]Lk. 10: 30.   [8]Lk. 15: 20.   [9]Lk. 16: 20; Ps. 54: 16; 70: 9.   [10]Lk. 10: 30.

The Priest saw me first, but passed by on the other side; the Levite looked on me in my distress, but despised my nakedness. O Jesus, sprung from Mary, do Thou come to me and take pity on me.[11]

O Lamb of God, that takest away the sins of all, take from me the heavy yoke of sin, and in Thy compassion grant me remission of sins.[12]

It is time for repentance: to Thee I come, my Creator. Take from me the heavy yoke of sin, and in Thy compassion grant me remission of sins.

Reject me not, O Saviour: cast me not away from Thy presence. Take from me the heavy yoke of sin and in Thy compassion grant me remission of sins.

All mine offences, voluntary and involuntary, manifest and hidden, known and unknown, do Thou forgive, O Saviour, for Thou art God; be merciful and save me.

From my youth, O Saviour, I have rejected Thy commandments. Ruled by the passions, I have passed my whole life in heedlessness and sloth. Therefore I cry to Thee, O Saviour, even now at the end: Save me.

As the Prodigal, O Saviour, I have wasted the substance of my soul in riotous living, and I am barren of the virtues of holiness. In my hunger I cry: O compassionate Father, come quickly out to meet me and take pity on me.[13]

I fall down, Jesus, at Thy feet: I have sinned against Thee, be merciful to me. Take from me the heavy yoke of sin, and in Thy compassion grant me tears of compunction.

Enter not into judgement with me, bringing before me the things I should have done, examining my words and correcting my impulses. But in Thy mercy overlook my sins and save me, O Lord almighty.[14]

ANOTHER CANON, OF SAINT MARY OF EGYPT
TO THE SAME TONE AND EIRMOS:

REFRAIN: *Holy mother Mary, pray to God for us.*

Give me the light of grace, from God's providence on high, that I may flee from the darkness of the passions and sing fervently the joyful story of thy life, O Mary.

REFRAIN: *Holy mother Mary, pray to God for us.*

Bowing before the divine laws of Christ, thou hast drawn near to Him, forsaking the unbridled longings of sensual pleasure; and in fear of God thou hast gained all the virtues as if they were one.

[11]Lk. 10: 31–33. [12]Jn. 1: 29. [13]Lk. 15:11–20. [14]Ps. 142: 2.

REFRAIN: *Holy father Andrew, pray to God for us.*

Through thine intercessions, Andrew, deliver us from shameful passions and, we pray thee, make us now partakers of Christ's Kingdom; for with faith and love we sing thy praises.

Glory to the Father, and to the Son, and to the Holy Spirit.

Trinity beyond all being, worshipped in Unity, take from me the heavy yoke of sin, and in Thy compassion grant me tears of compunction.

Both now and ever, and unto the ages of ages. Amen.

O Theotokos, the hope and protection of those who sing thy praises, take from me the heavy yoke of sin and, pure Lady, accept me in repentance.

Ode 2

EIRMOS: *Attend, O heaven, and I shall speak and sing in praise of Christ, who took flesh from a Virgin and came to dwell among us.*

REFRAIN: *Have mercy on me, O God, have mercy on me.*

Attend, O heaven, and I shall speak; give ear, O earth, to the voice of one who repents before God and sings His praise.[15]

Look upon me in compassion, O God, with Thy merciful eye, and accept my fervent confession.

More than all men have I sinned; I alone have sinned against Thee. But as God take pity on Thy creation, O Saviour.

I am surrounded by the storm of sin, O compassionate Lord. But stretch out Thine hand to me, as once Thou hast to Peter.[16]

I offer to Thee, O merciful Lord, the tears of the Harlot. Take pity on me, O Saviour, in Thy compassion.[17]

With the lusts of passion I have darkened the beauty of my soul, and turned my whole mind entirely into dust

I have torn the first garment that the Creator wove for me in the beginning, and now I lie naked.

I have clothed myself in the torn coat that the serpent wove for me by his counsel, and I am ashamed.

I looked upon the beauty of the tree and my mind was deceived; and now I lie naked and ashamed.[18]

---

[15]Deut. 32:1.   [16]Matt. 14: 31.   [17]Lk. 7: 38.   [18]Gen. 3: 7.

All the ruling passions have ploughed upon my back, making long fur-rows of wickedness.[19]

I have lost the beauty and glory with which I was first created; and now I lie naked and ashamed.

Sin has stripped me of the robe that God once wove for me, and it has sewed for me garments of skin.[20]

I am clothed with the raiment of shame as with fig leaves, in condemna-tion of my self-willed passions.[21]

I am clad in a garment that is defiled and shamefully blood-stained by a life of passion and self-indulgence..

I have stained the garment of my flesh, O Saviour, and defiled that which was made in Thine image and likeness.

I have fallen beneath the painful burden of the passions and the corrup-tion of material things; and I am hard pressed by the enemy.

Instead of freedom from possessions, O Saviour, I have pursued a life in love with material things; and now I wear a heavy yoke.

I have adorned the idol of my flesh with a many-colored coat of shameful thoughts, and I am condemned.

I have cared only for the outward adornment, and neglected that which is within—the tabernacle fashioned by God.

With my lustful desires I have formed within myself the deformity of the passions and disfigured the beauty of my mind.

I have discoloured with the passions the first beauty of the image, O Sav-iour. But seek me, as once Thou hast sought the lost coin, and find me.[22]

Like the Harlot I cry to Thee: I have sinned, I alone have sinned against Thee. Accept my tears also as sweet ointment, O Saviour.[23]

Like David, I have fallen into lust and I am covered with filth; but wash me clean, O Saviour, by my tears.[24]

Like the Publican I cry to Thee: Be merciful, O Saviour, be merciful to me. For no child of Adam has ever sinned against Thee as I have sinned.[25]

I have no tears, no repentance, no compunction; but as God do Thou Thyself, O Saviour, bestow them on me.

Lord, Lord, at the Last Day shut not Thy door against me; but open it to me, for I repent before Thee.[26]

---

[19]Ps. 128: 3.   [20]Gen. 3: 21.   [21]Gen. 3: 7.   [22]Lk. 15: 8.
[23]Lk. 7: 37–50.   [24]2 Kgs. [2 Sam]11: 2–4.   [25]Lk. 18: 13.   [26]Matt. 25: 11.

O Lover of mankind, who desirest that all men shall be saved, in Thy goodness call me back and accept me in repentance.[27]

Give ear to the groaning of my soul, and accept the tears that fall from mine eyes: O Saviour, save me.

Most holy Theotokos, save us.

O Theotokos undefiled, Virgin alone worthy of all praise, intercede fervently for our salvation.

ANOTHER EIRMOS: *See now, see that I am God, who rained down manna in the days of old, and made springs of water flow from the rock, for My people in the wilderness, by My right hand and by My power alone.*

REFRAIN: *Have mercy on me, O God, have mercy on me.*

'See now, see that I am God': give ear, my soul, to the Lord as He cries to thee. Forsake thy former sin, and fear Him as thy judge and God.

To whom shall I liken thee, O soul of many sins? Alas! to Cain and to Lamech. For thou hast stoned thy body to death with thine evil deeds, and killed thy mind with thy disordered longings.[28]

Call to mind, my soul, all who lived before the Law. Thou hast not been like Seth, or followed Enos or Enoch, who was translated to heaven, or Noah; but thou art found destitute, without a share in the life of the righteous.[29]

Thou alone, my soul, hast opened the windows of the wrath of thy God, and thou hast flooded, as the earth, all thy flesh and deeds and life; and thou hast remained outside the Ark of salvation.[30]

'I have slain a man to my grief and wounding', said Lamech, 'and a young man to my hurt'; and he cried aloud lamenting. Dost thou not tremble then, my soul, for thou hast defiled thy flesh and polluted thy mind?[31]

Ah, how I have emulated Lamech, the murderer of old, slaying my soul as if it were a man, and my mind as if it were a young man. With sensual longings I have killed my body, as Cain the murderer killed his brother.[32]

Skilfully hast thou planned to build a tower, O my soul, and to establish a stronghold for thy lusts; but the Creator confounded thy designs and dashed thy devices to the ground.[33]

I am wounded and smitten; see the enemy's arrows which have pierced my soul and body. See the wounds, the open sores and the injuries, I cry to Thee; see the blows inflicted by my freely-chosen passions.

[27]1 Tim. 2: 4.   [28]Gen. 4: 8, 23.   [29]Gen. 5:3, 6, 21–24; 6: 9.
[30]Gen. 7: 11–13.   [31]Gen. 4: 23.   [32]Gen. 4: 23; 4:6–8.   [33]Gen. 11: 3–8.

Roused to anger by their transgressions, the Lord once rained down fire from heaven and burnt up the men of Sodom. And thou, my soul, hast kindled the fire of Gehenna, and there to thy bitter sorrow thou shalt burn.[34]

Know and see that I am God, searching out men's hearts and punishing their thoughts, reproving their actions and burning up their sins; and in My judgement I protect the orphan and the humble and the poor.[35]

REFRAIN: *Holy mother Mary, pray to God for us.*

Sunk in the abyss of wickedness, O Mary, thou hast lifted up thine hands to the merciful God. And, as to Peter, in His loving-kindness He stretched out His hand to thee in help, seeking in every way thy conversion.[36]

REFRAIN: *Holy mother Mary, pray to God for us.*

With all eagerness and love thou hast run to Christ, turning from thy former path of sin, finding thy food in the trackless wilderness, and fulfilling in purity the commandments of God.

REFRAIN: *Holy father Andrew, pray to God for us.*

Let us see, O my soul, let us see the love of our God and Master for mankind; and before the end comes, with tears let us fall down before Him, crying: At the prayers of Andrew, O Saviour, have mercy upon us.

Glory to the Father, and to the Son, and to the Holy Spirit.

O Trinity uncreated and without beginning, O undivided Unity: accept me in repentance and save me, a sinner. I am Thy creation, reject me not; but spare me and deliver me from the fire of condemnation.

Both now and ever, and unto the ages of ages. Amen.

Most pure Lady, Mother of God, the hope of those who run to thee and the haven of the storm-tossed: pray to the merciful God, thy Creator and thy Son, that He may grant His mercy even to me.

Ode 3

EIRMOS: *Upon the unshaken rock of Thy commandments, O Christ, make firm Thy Church.*

REFRAIN: *Have mercy on me, O God, have mercy on me.*

The Lord, my soul, once rained down fire from heaven and consumed the land of Sodom.[37]

---

[34]Gen. 19: 24; Matt. 5:22.   [35]Deut. 10: 18; Ps. 67: 6.   [36]Matt 14: 31.   [37]Gen. 19: 24.

O my soul, flee like Lot to the mountain, and take refuge in Zoar before it is too late.

Flee from the flames, my soul, flee from the burning heat of Sodom, flee from destruction by the fire of God.[38]

I confess to Thee, O Saviour; I have sinned, I have sinned against Thee. But in Thy compassion absolve and forgive me.

I alone have sinned against Thee, I have sinned more than all men; reject me not, O Christ my Saviour.

Thou art the Good Shepherd: seek me, the lamb that has strayed, and do not forget me.[39]

Thou art my beloved Jesus, Thou art my Creator; in Thee shall I be justified, O Saviour.

Most Holy Trinity, our God, Glory to Thee.

O God, Trinity in Unity, save us from error and temptation and distress.

Most holy Theotokos, save us.

Hail, Womb that held God! Hail, Throne of the Lord! Hail, Mother of our life!

ANOTHER EIRMOS: *O Lord, upon the rock of Thy commandments make firm my wavering heart, for Thou alone art Holy and Lord.*

REFRAIN: *Have mercy on me, O God, have mercy on me.*

For me Thou art the Fountain of life and the Destroyer of death; and from my heart I cry to Thee before the end: I have sinned, be merciful to me and save me.[40]

I have followed the example, O Saviour, of those who lived in wantonness in the days of Noah; and like them I am condemned to drown in the flood.[41]

I have sinned, O Lord, I have sinned against Thee; be merciful to me. For there is no sinner whom I have not surpassed in my offences.

O my soul, thou hast followed Ham, who mocked his father. Thou hast not covered thy neighbour's shame, walking backwards with averted face.[42]

O wretched soul, thou hast not inherited the blessing of Shem, nor hast thou received, like Japhet, a spacious domain in the land of forgiveness.[43]

---

[38]Deut. 4: 24; Heb. 12: 29.   [39]Jn. 10: 11–14; Lk. 15:4–6.   [40]Ps. 35: 10; Jn. 4: 14; 7: 37.
[41]Gen. 6:5 –13; Matt. 24:37–39.   [42]Gen. 9: 20–27.   [43]Gen. 9: 26–27.

O my soul, depart from sin, from the land of Haran, and come to the land that Abraham inherited, which flows with incorruption and eternal life.[44]

Thou hast heard, my soul, how Abraham in days of old left the land of his fathers and became a wanderer: follow him in his choice.[45]

At the oak of Mamre the Patriarch gave hospitality to the angels, and in his old age he inherited the reward of the promise.[46]

Thou knowest, O my miserable soul, how Isaac was offered mystically as a new and unwonted sacrifice to the Lord: follow him in his choice.[47]

Thou hast heard—O my soul, be watchful! —how Ishmael was driven out as the child of a bondwoman. Take heed, lest the same thing happen to thee because of thy lust.[48]

O my soul, thou hast become like Hagar the Egyptian: thy free choice has been enslaved, and thou hast borne as thy child a new Ishmael, stubborn wilfulness.[49]

Thou knowest, my soul, the ladder that was shown to Jacob, reaching up from earth to heaven. Why hast thou not provided a firm foundation for it through thy godly actions?[50]

Follow the example of Melchizedek, the priest of God, the King set apart, who was an image of the life of Christ among men in the world.[51]

Do not look back, my soul, and so be turned into a pillar of salt. Fear the example of the people of Sodom, and take refuge in Zoar.[52]

Flee, my soul, like Lot, from the burning of sin; flee from Sodom and Gomorrah; flee from the flame of every brutish desire.[53]

Have mercy, O Lord, have mercy on me, I cry to Thee, when Thou comest with Thine angels to give to every man due return for his deeds.

Reject not, O Master, the prayer of those who sing Thy praises, but in Thy loving-kindness be merciful and grant forgiveness to them that ask with faith.

REFRAIN: *Holy mother Mary, pray to God for us.*

I am held fast, O Mother, by the tempest and billows of sin: but do thou keep me safe and lead me to the haven of divine repentance.

REFRAIN: *Holy mother Mary, pray to God for us.*

O holy Mary, offer thy prayer of supplication to the compassionate Theotokos, and through thine intercessions open unto me the door that leads to God.

---

[44]Gen. 11:31–12:1; Exod.3:8.   [45]Gen. 12: 1.   [46]Gen. 18: 1–15.
[47]Gen. 22: 1–14.   [48]Gen. 21: 10.   [49]Gen. 16: 3, 15.   [50]Gen. 28: 12.
[51]Gen. 14: 18; Heb. 7: 1–3.   [52]Gen. 19: 23, 26.   [53]Gen. 19:17–25.

REFRAIN: *Holy father Andrew, pray to God for us.*

Through thy prayers grant even to me forgiveness of trespasses, O Andrew, Bishop of Crete, best of guides, leading us to the mysteries of repentance.

Glory to the Father, and to the Son, and to the Holy Spirit.

O simple Unity praised in Trinity of Persons, uncreated Nature without beginning, save us who in faith worship Thy power.

Both now and ever, and unto the ages of ages. Amen.

O Mother of God, without knowing man thou hast given birth within time to the Son, who was begotten outside time from the Father; and, strange wonder! thou givest suck while still remaining Virgin.

AND AGAIN THE EIRMOS: *O Lord, upon the rock of Thy commandments make firm my wavering heart, for Thou alone art Holy and Lord.*

LITTLE LITANY: Again and again in peace . . .

EXCLAMATION: For Thou art our God . . .

SEDALION · TONE 8 · THE WORK OF JOSEPH

Divinely-shining lights, eyewitnesses of the Saviour, illuminate us in the darkness of this life, that we may now walk honestly as in the day; with the torch of abstinence may we drive out the passions of the night, and behold with joy the splendour of Christ's Passion.[54]

Glory to the Father, and to the Son, and to the Holy Spirit.

ANOTHER · THE WORK OF THEODORE

O company of the twelve apostles, chosen by God, offer now to Christ your supplication, that we may all complete the course of the Fast, saying our prayers with compunction and practising the virtues with an eager heart; and so may we attain the glorious Resurrection of Christ our God, bringing to Him praise and glory.

Both now and ever, and unto the ages of ages. Amen.

The Son and Word of God whom nothing can contain, in ways past speech and understanding was born from thee, O Theotokos. With the apostles pray to Him, that He may bestow true peace upon the inhabited earth and grant to us before the end forgiveness of our sins, in His boundless love counting thy servants worthy of the heavenly Kingdom.

[54]Rom.13: 13.

The Second half of the Life of Saint Mary of Egypt is read here.
Then, the following Triode canon is read, omitting the eirmoi.

TRIODION OR THREE ODES (WITHOUT BOWS)
THE WORK OF JOSEPH

Ode 4 · Tone 8

EIRMOS: *O Lord, I have heard the mystery of Thy dispensation: I have considered Thy works, and I have glorified Thy Godhead.*

REFRAIN: *Holy Apostles, pray to God for us.*

Enlightened by God, the apostles of Christ lived in abstinence; and by their divine mediation they help us in this season of the Fast.

As an instrument of twelve strings, the divine choir of the disciples sang a hymn of salvation, confounding the music of evil.

Driving away the drought of polytheism, O all-blessed apostles, with the rain of the Spirit ye have watered all the earth.

Most holy Theotokos, save us

I have passed my life in arrogance: make me humble and save me, all-pure Lady, for thou hast borne the Lord who has exalted our humiliated nature.

ANOTHER TRIODION · THE WORK OF THEODORE

EIRMOS: *I have heard the report of Thee, O Lord, and was afraid; I have considered Thy works and glorified Thy power, O Master.*

REFRAIN: *Holy Apostles, pray to God for us.*

O honoured choir of the apostles, in your intercessions to the Maker of all, ask that He have mercy on us who sing your praises.

As Christ's husbandmen, O apostles, ye have tilled the whole world with the word of God, and ye bring Him fruit at all times.

Ye became a vineyard, O apostles, for Christ the well-beloved, and ye have made all the world to drink from the wine of the Spirit.[55]

Most Holy Trinity, our God, Glory to Thee.

Trinity one in essence, without beginning and supreme in power, Father, Son and Holy Spirit: O God, Light and Life, guard Thy flock.

Most Holy Theotokos, save us.

[55]Isa. 5:1.

Hail, fiery Throne! Hail, Candlestick that bears the Light! Hail, Mountain of sanctification, Ark of life, Tabernacle and Holy of Holies![56]

CONTINUATION OF THE GREAT CANON

Ode 4

EIRMOS: *The prophet heard of Thy coming, O Lord, and he was afraid: how Thou wast to be born of a Virgin and revealed to men, and he said: 'I have heard the report of Thee and I was afraid.' Glory to Thy power, O Lord.*
REFRAIN: *Have mercy on me, O God, have mercy on me.*

O righteous Judge, despise not Thy works; forsake not Thy creation. I have sinned as a man, I alone, more than any other man, O Thou who lovest mankind. But as Lord of all Thou hast the power to pardon sins.[57]

The end draws near, my soul, the end draws near; yet thou dost not care or make ready. The time grows short, rise up: the Judge is at the door. The days of our life pass swiftly, as a dream, as a flower. Why do we trouble ourselves in vain?[58]

Awake, my soul, consider the actions which thou hast done; set them before thine eyes, and let the drops of thy tears fall. With boldness tell Christ of thy deeds and thoughts, and so be justified.

No sin has there been in life, no evil deed, no wickedness, that I have not committed, O Saviour. I have sinned as no one ever before, in mind, word and intent, in disposition, thought and act.

For this I am condemned in my misery, for this I am convicted by the verdict of my own conscience, which is more compelling than all else in the world. O my Judge and Redeemer, who knowest my heart, spare and deliver and save me Thy servant.

The ladder which the great Patriarch Jacob saw of old is an example, O my soul, of approach through action and of ascent in knowledge. If then thou dost wish to live rightly in action and knowledge and contemplation, be thou made new.[59]

In privation Jacob the Patriarch endured the burning heat by day and the frost by night, making daily gains of sheep and cattle, shepherding, wrestling and serving, to win his two wives.[60]

---

[56]Dan. 7: 9; Exod 25: 31–7; Ps. 77: 54; Exod. 25: 10; 26: 1, 33.
[57]Mk. 2: 10.   [58]Matt. 24: 33; Ps. 38: 7.
[59]Gen. 28:12.   [60]Gen. 29: 16–30, 30:31–33; 31:38–41.

By the two wives, understand action and knowledge in contemplation. Leah is action, for she had many children; and Rachel is knowledge, for she endured great toil. And without toil, O my soul, neither action nor contemplation will succeed.

Be watchful, O my soul, be full of courage like Jacob the great Patriarch, that thou mayest acquire action with knowledge, and be named 'Israel', 'the mind that sees God'; so shalt thou reach by contemplation the innermost darkness, and gain great merchandise.[61]

The great Patriarch had the twelve Patriarchs as children, and so he mystically established for thee, my soul, a ladder of ascent through action, in his wisdom setting his children as steps, by which thou canst mount upwards.[62]

Thou hast rivalled Esau the hated, O my soul, and given the birthright of thy first beauty to the supplanter; thou hast lost thy father's blessing and in thy wretchedness been twice supplanted, in action and in knowledge. Therefore repent now.[63]

Esau was called Edom because of his raging lust for women; burning always with unrestrained desires and stained with sensual pleasure, he was named 'Edom', which means the red heat of a soul that loves sin.[64]

Thou hast heard, O my soul, of Job justified on a dung-hill, but thou hast not imitated his fortitude. In all thine experiences and trials and temptations, thou hast not kept firmly to thy purpose but hast proved inconstant.[65]

Once he sat upon a throne, but now he sits upon a dung-hill, naked and covered with sores. Once he was blessed with many children and admired by all, but suddenly he is childless and homeless. Yet he counted the dung-hill as a palace and his sores as pearls.

A man of great wealth and righteous, abounding in riches and cattle, clothed in royal dignity, in crown and purple robe, Job became suddenly a beggar, stripped of wealth, glory and kingship.[66]

If he who was righteous and blameless above all men did not escape the snares and pits of the deceiver, what wilt thou do, wretched and sin-loving soul, when some sudden misfortune befalls thee?[67]

I have defiled my body, I have stained my spirit, and I am all covered with wounds: but as physician, O Christ, heal both body and spirit for me through repentance. Wash, purify and cleanse me, O my Saviour, and make me whiter than snow.

[61]Gen. 32: 28–30.　[62]Gen 28: 12–14; 35: 22.　[63]Gen. 25: 31; 27: 37.　[64]Gen. 25:30.　[65]Job 2: 8–10.　[66]Job 1: 1–22.　[67]Job 2: 3–6.

Thy Body and Thy Blood, O Word, Thou hast offered at Thy Crucifixion for the sake of all: Thy Body to refashion me, Thy Blood to wash me clean; and Thou hast given up Thy spirit, O Christ, to bring me to Thy Father.[68]

O Creator, Thou hast worked salvation in the midst of the earth, that we might be saved. Thou wast crucified of Thine own will upon the Tree; and Eden, closed till then, was opened. Things above and things below, the creation and all peoples have been saved and worship Thee.[69]

May the Blood from Thy side be to me a cleansing fount, and may the water that flows with it be a drink of forgiveness. May I be purified by both, O Word, anointed and refreshed, having as chrism and drink Thy words of life.[70]

I am deprived of the bridal chamber, of the wedding and the supper; for want of oil my lamp has gone out; while I slept the door was closed; the supper has been eaten; I am bound hand and foot, and cast out.[71]

As a chalice, O my Saviour, the Church has been granted Thy life-giving side, from which there flows down to us a twofold stream of forgiveness and knowledge, representing the two covenants, the Old and the New.[72]

The time of my life is short, filled with trouble and evil. But accept me in repentance and call me back to knowledge. Let me not become the possession and food of the enemy; but do Thou, O Saviour, take pity on me.

Now I speak boastfully, with boldness of heart; yet all to no purpose and in vain. O righteous Judge, who alone art compassionate, do not condemn me with the Pharisee; but grant me the abasement of the Publican and number me with him.[73]

I know, O compassionate Lord, that I have sinned and violated the vessel of my flesh. But accept me in repentance and call me back to knowledge. Let me not become the possession and food of the enemy; but do Thou, O Saviour, take pity on me.

I have become mine own idol, utterly defiling my soul with the passions, O compassionate Lord. But accept me in repentance and call me back to knowledge. Let me not become the possession and food of the enemy; but do Thou, O Saviour, take pity on me.

---

[68]Lk. 23: 46.   [69]Ps. 73:12.   [70]Jn. 6:55, 19: 34.
[71]Matt. 25; Lk. 14: 7–35; Matt. 22: 1–14.
[72]Ex.. 24: 8; Matt. 26: 28; Jn. 19: 34.   [73]Lk. 18: 9–14.

I have not hearkened to Thy voice, I have not heeded Thy Scripture, O Giver of the Law. But accept me in repentance and call me back to knowledge. Let me not become the possession and food of the enemy; but do Thou, O Saviour, take pity on me.

REFRAIN: *Holy mother Mary, pray to God for us.*

Thou hast lived a bodiless life in the body, O holy Mary, and thou hast received great grace from God. Protect us who honour thee with faith and, we entreat thee, deliver us by thy prayers from every trial.

REFRAIN: *Holy mother Mary, pray to God for us.*

Thou wast brought down into an abyss of great iniquity, yet not held fast within it: but with better intent thou hast mounted through action to the height of virtue, past all expectation; and the angels, O Mary, were amazed at thee.

REFRAIN: *Holy father Andrew, pray to God for us.*

O Andrew, renowned among the fathers, glory of Crete, as thou standest before the Trinity supreme in Godhead, in thy prayers do not forget to ask that we may be delivered from torment: for we call upon thee with love as our advocate in heaven.

Glory to the Father, and to the Son, and to the Holy Spirit.

Undivided in Essence, unconfused in Persons, I confess Thee as God: Triune Deity, one in kingship and throne; and to Thee I raise the great thrice-holy hymn that is sung on high.[74]

Both now and ever, and unto the ages of ages. Amen.

Thou givest birth and art a virgin, and in both thou remainest by nature inviolate. He who is born makes new the laws of nature, and thy womb brings forth without travail. When God so wills, the natural order is overcome; for He does whatever He wishes.

Ode 5

EIRMOS: *From the night I seek Thee early, O Lover of mankind: give me light, I pray Thee, and guide me in Thy commandments, and teach me, O Saviour, to do Thy will.*

REFRAIN: *Have mercy on me, O God, have mercy on me.*

---

[74]Isa. 6: 3; Rev. 4: 8.

In night have I passed all my life: for the night of sin has covered me with darkness and thick mist. But make me, O Saviour, a son of the day.[75]

In my misery I have followed Reuben's example, and have devised a wicked and unlawful plan against the most high God, defiling my bed as he defiled his father's.[76]

I confess to Thee, O Christ my King: I have sinned, I have sinned like the brethren of Joseph, who once sold the fruit of purity and chastity.[77]

As a figure of the Lord, O my soul, the righteous and gentle Joseph was sold into bondage by his brethren; but thou hast sold thyself entirely to thy sins.

O miserable and wicked soul, imitate the righteous and pure mind of Joseph; and do not live in wantonness, sinfully indulging thy disordered desires.[78]

Once Joseph was cast into a pit, O Lord and Master, as a figure of Thy Burial and Resurrection. But what offering such as this shall I ever make to Thee?[79]

Thou hast heard, my soul, of the basket of Moses: how he was borne on the waves of the river as if in a shrine; and so he avoided the bitter execution of Pharaoh's decree.[80]

Thou hast heard, wretched soul, of the midwives who once killed in its infancy the manly action of self-control: like great Moses, then, be suckled on wisdom.[81]

O miserable soul, thou hast not struck and killed the Egyptian mind, as did Moses the great. Tell me, then, how wilt thou go to dwell through repentance in the wilderness empty of passions?[82]

Moses the great went to dwell in the desert. Come, seek to follow his way of life, my soul, that in contemplation thou mayest attain the vision of God in the bush.[83]

Picture to thyself, my soul, the rod of Moses striking the sea and making hard the deep by the sign of the Holy Cross. Through the Cross thou also canst do great things.[84]

Aaron offered to God fire that was blameless and undefiled, but Hophni and Phinehas brought to Him, as thou hast done, my soul, strange fire and a polluted life.[85]

---

[75]Eph. 5: 8; Thess. 5:5.   [76]Gen. 35: 22, 49: 3–4.   [77]Gen. 37:27–28.
[78]Gen. 39: 7–20.   [79]Gen. 37:24.   [80]Ex. 1: 22–2: 3.   [81]Ex. 1: 16; 2–9.
[82]Ex. 2: 12.   [83]Ex. 3: 1–6.   [84]Ex. 14: 16.   [85]Num. 16: 1–40; 1 Kgs.[1Sam] 2: 12–34.

In my soul and body, O Master, I have become like Jannes and Jambres the magicians of cruel Pharaoh; my will is heavy and my mind is drowned beneath the waters. But do Thou come to my aid.[86]

Woe is me! I have defiled my mind with filth. I pray to Thee, O Master: wash me clean in the waters of my tears and make the garment of my flesh white as snow.

When I examine my actions, O Saviour, I see that I have gone beyond all men in sin; for I knew and understood what I did; I was not sinning in ignorance.

Spare, O spare the work of Thine hands, O Lord. I have sinned, forgive me: for Thou alone art pure by nature, and none save Thee is free from defilement.[87]

Thou who art God, O Saviour, wast for my sake fashioned as I am. Thou hast performed miracles, healing lepers, giving strength to the paralysed, stopping the issue of blood when the woman touched the hem of Thy garment.[88]

O wretched soul, do as the woman with an issue of blood: run quickly, grasp the hem of the garment of Christ; so shalt thou be healed of thine afflictions and hear Him say, 'Thy faith has saved thee.'[89]

O my soul, do as the woman who was bowed to the ground. Fall at the feet of Jesus, that He may make thee straight again: and thou shalt walk upright upon the paths of the Lord.[90]

Thou art a deep well, O Master: make springs gush forth for me from Thy pure veins, that like the woman of Samaria I may drink and thirst no more; for from Thee flow the streams of life.[91]

O Master and Lord, may my tears be unto me as Siloam: that I also may wash clean the eyes of my soul, and with my mind behold Thee, the pre-eternal Light.[92]

REFRAIN: *Holy mother Mary, pray to God for us.*

O blessed saint, with a love beyond compare thou hast longed to venerate the Wood of life, and thy desire was granted. Make me also worthy to attain the glory on high.

REFRAIN: *Holy mother Mary, pray to God for us.*

Crossing the stream of Jordan, thou hast found peace, escaping from the deadening pleasures of the flesh. Deliver us also from them, holy Mary, by thine intercessions.

[86]Exod. 7: 11; 2 Tim. 3: 8. [87]1 Pet. 3.21.
[88]Phil. 2:6; Matt. 4: 24; Lk. 5:18, 8: 43–44, 17:12–14.
[89]Matt. 9:20–22. [90]Lk. 13: 11–13. [91]Jn. 4: 13–15. [92]Jn. 9: 7.

REFRAIN: *Holy father Andrew, pray to God for us.*

Best of shepherds, chosen above all others, O wise Andrew, with great love and fear I beseech thee: through thine intercessions may I receive salvation and eternal life.

Glory to the Father, and to the Son, and to the Holy Spirit.

We glorify Thee, O Trinity, the one God. Holy, holy, holy art Thou: Father, Son and Spirit, simple Essence and Unity, worshipped for ever.

Both now and ever, and unto the ages of ages. Amen.

O Virgin inviolate and Mother who hast not known man, from thee has God, the Creator of the ages, taken human flesh, uniting to Himself the nature of men.

Ode 6

EIRMOS: *With my whole heart I cried to the all-compassionate God: and He heard me from the lowest depths of hell, and brought my life out of corruption.*
REFRAIN: *Have mercy on me, O God, have mercy on me.*

I offer to Thee in purity, O Saviour, the tears of mine eyes and groanings from the depths of my heart, crying: 'I have sinned against Thee, O God; be merciful to me.'[93]

Like Dathan and Abiram, O my soul, thou hast become a stranger to Thy Lord; but with all thy heart cry out, 'Spare me', that the earth may not open and swallow thee up.[94]

Raging as a maddened heifer, O my soul, thou art become like Ephraim. As a hart from the nets rescue then thy life, gaining wings through action and the mind's contemplation.[95]

O my soul, the hand of Moses shall be our assurance, proving that God can cleanse a life full of leprosy and make it white as snow. So do not despair of thyself, though thou art leprous.[96]

The waves of my sins, O Saviour, have returned and suddenly engulfed me, as the waters of the Red Sea engulfed the Egyptians of old and their charioteers.[97]

Like Israel before thee, thou hast made a foolish choice, my soul; instead of the divine manna thou hast senselessly preferred the pleasure-loving gluttony of the passions.[98]

[93]Lk. 18:13.   [94]Num. 16:32.   [95]Hos. 10:11.
[96]Ex. 4: 6–8.   [97]Ex. 14: 7–31.   [98]Ex. 16:15; Num. 21: 5; 1.

O my soul, thou hast valued the wells of Canaanite thoughts more than the veined Rock, Jesus, the Fountain of wisdom from which flow the rivers of divine knowledge.[99]

The swine's meat, the flesh-pots and the food of Egypt thou hast preferred, my soul, to the food of heaven, as the ungrateful people did of old in the wilderness.[100]

When Thy servant Moses struck the rock with his rod, he prefigured Thy life-giving side, O Saviour, from which we all draw the water of life.[101]

Like Joshua the son of Nun, search and spy out, my soul, the land of thine inheritance and take up thy dwelling within it, through obedience to the law.[102]

Rise up and make war against the passions of the flesh, as Joshua against Amalek, ever gaining the victory over the Gibeonites, thy deceitful thoughts.[103]

O my soul, pass through the flowing waters of time like the Ark of old, and take possession of the land of promise: for God commands thee.[104]

As Thou hast saved Peter when he cried out, 'Save me', come quickly, O Saviour, before it is too late, and save me from the beast. Stretch out Thine hand and lead me up from the deep of sin.[105]

I know Thee as a calm haven, O Lord, Lord Christ: come quickly, before it is too late, and deliver me from the lowest depths of sin and despair.

O Saviour, I am the coin marked with the King's likeness, which Thou hast lost of old. But, O Word, light Thy lamp, Thy Forerunner, and seek and find again Thine image.[106]

REFRAIN: *Holy mother Mary, pray to God for us.*

Thy soul on fire, O Mary, thou hast ever shed streams of tears, to quench the burning of the passions. Grant the grace of these thy tears to me also, thy servant.

REFRAIN: *Holy mother Mary, pray to God for us.*

Through the perfection of thine earthly life, O Mother, thou hast gained a heavenly freedom from the sinfulness of passion. In thine intercessions pray that this same freedom may be given to those who sing thy praises.

REFRAIN: *Holy father Andrew, pray to God for us.*

---

[99]Ex. 17:6; Num. 20:8; 2 Kgs. [2Sam]22:2; 1Cor. 10:4.   [100]Ex. 16:3; Num. 11:4–7.
[101]Ex. 17:6; Num. 20: 11; Jn. 19:34; 1 Cor. 10: 4.   [102]Num. 13:21–25, 14:30; Josh. 2:1.
[103]Ex.17: 8; Josh. 8: 21.   [104]Ex.17: 8–13; Josh. 9: 3–27.   [105]Matt. 14: 25–31.
[106]Lk. 15: 8; Jn.5:35.

Shepherd and bishop of Crete, intercessor for the inhabited earth, to thee I run, O Andrew, and I cry: 'Deliver me, father, from the depths of sin.'

Glory to the Father, and to the Son, and to the Holy Spirit.

'I am the Trinity, simple and undivided, yet divided in Persons, and I am the Unity, by Nature one', says the Father and the Son and the divine Spirit.

Both now and ever, and unto the ages of ages. Amen.

Thy womb bore God for us, fashioned in our shape. O Theotokos, pray to Him as the Creator of all, that we may be justified through thine intercessions.

AND AGAIN THE EIRMOS: *With my whole heart I cried to the all-compassionate God: and He heard me from the lowest depths of hell, and brought my life out of corruption.*

LITTLE LITANY: Again and again in peace . . .

EXCLAMATION: For Thou art the King of Peace and the Saviour of our souls . . . CHOIR: *Amen.*

KONTAKION · TONE 6

My soul, O my soul, rise up! Why art thou sleeping? The end draws near, and soon thou shalt be troubled. Watch, then, that Christ thy God may spare thee, for He is everywhere present and fills all things.

EIKOS

Seeing Christ's house of healing opened, and health flowing down from it upon Adam, the devil suffered and was wounded; and as one in mortal danger he lamented, crying to his friends: 'What shall I do to the Son of Mary? I am slain by the Man from Bethlehem, who is everywhere present and fills all things.'

Then we sing the Beatitudes and the Troparia as follows, with one bow at each, tone 6:

In Thy Kingdom remember us, O Lord, when Thou comest in Thy Kingdom.

O Christ, when the Thief cried to Thee upon the Cross 'Remember me', Thou hast made him a citizen of Paradise. Unworthy though I am, grant me to repent like him.[107]

Blessed are the poor in spirit, for theirs is the Kingdom of Heaven.

---

[107]Lk. 23: 42–43.

O my soul, thou hast heard how Manoah of old beheld the Lord in a vision, and then received from his barren wife the fruit of God's promise. Let us imitate him in his devotion.[108]

Blessed are those who mourn, for they shall be comforted.

Emulating Samson's slothfulness, O my soul, thou hast been shorn of the glory of thy works, and through love of pleasure thou hast betrayed thy life to the alien Philistines, surrendering thy chastity and blessedness.[109]

Blessed are the meek, for they shall inherit the earth.

He who at the first overthrew the Philistines with the jawbone of an ass, then wasted his life in passionate lusts. Flee, O my soul, from his example, flee from his actions and his weakness.

Blessed are those who hunger and thirst for righteousness, for they shall be filled.

Barak and Jepthah the captains, with Deborah who had a man's courage, were chosen as judges of Israel. Learn bravery from their mighty acts, O my soul, and be strong.[110]

Blessed are the merciful, for they shall obtain mercy.

O my soul, thou knowest the manly courage of Jael, who of old pierced Sisera through his temples and brought salvation to Israel with the nail of her tent. In this thou mayest see a prefiguring of the Cross.[111]

Blessed are the pure in heart, for they shall see God.

Offer, my soul, a sacrifice worthy of praise, offer thine actions as an oblation purer than the daughter of Jepthah; and as a victim for thy Lord slay the passions of the flesh.[112]

Blessed are the peacemakers, for they shall be called children of God.

O my soul, consider the fleece of Gideon, and receive the dew from heaven; bend down like a hart[113]and drink the water that flows from the Law, when its letter is wrung out for thee through study.[114]

Blessed are those who are persecuted for righteousness' sake, for theirs is the Kingdom of Heaven.

Thou hast drawn upon thyself, O my soul, the condemnation of Eli the priest: thoughtlessly thou hast allowed the passions to work evil within thee, just as he permitted his children to commit transgressions.[115]

---

[108]Judg. 13:2–24.   [109]Judg. 16:19–21.   [110]Judg. 4:4–6; 11:1.   [111]Judg. 4:21..
[112]Judg. 11:31, 39.   [113]Some editions read, 'like a dog'.
[114]Judg. 6:38; 7: 5–7; Ps.41:2.   [115]1 Kgs. [1Sam.] 2:12–25.

Blessed are you when men revile you, and persecute you, and say all manner of evil against you falsely and on My account.

In the Book of Judges, my soul, the Levite divided his wife limb from limb and sent the parts to the twelve tribes; and so he made known the lawless outrage committed by the men of Benjamin.[116]

Rejoice and be exceedingly glad, for great is your reward in Heaven.

Hannah, who loved self-restraint and chastity, when speaking to God moved her lips in praise, but her voice was not heard; and she who was barren bore a son worthy of her prayer.[117]

Remember us, O Lord, when Thou comest in Thy Kingdom.

Great Samuel, the son of Hannah, was born at Ramah and brought up in the house of the Lord; and he was numbered among the Judges of Israel. Eagerly follow his example, O my soul, and before thou judgest others, judge thine own works.[118]

Remember us, O Master, when Thou comest in Thy Kingdom.

David was chosen to be king and anointed for his royal office with the horn of divine oil. If thou, my soul, desirest the Kingdom on high, anoint thyself with the oil of tears.[119]

Remember us, O Holy One, when Thou comest in Thy Kingdom.

Have mercy upon Thy creation, merciful Lord; take pity on the work of Thy hands. Spare those who have sinned, and spare me who more than all others have despised Thy commandments.

Glory to the Father, and to the Son, and to the Holy. Spirit.

Without beginning are the birth of the Son and the procession of the Spirit. I worship the Father who begets, I glorify the Son who is begotten, and I sing the praises of the Holy Spirit who shines forth with the Father and the Son.

Both now and ever, and unto the ages of ages. Amen.

O Mother of God, we venerate thy childbearing in ways past nature, yet we do not divide in two the natural glory of thy Son: for He is confessed as one Person in two Natures.

---

[116]Judg. 19:29–30.   [117]1 Kgs. [1Sam.] 1:13, 20.
[118]1 Kgs. [1Sam.] 1:19; 2:11; 7:15.   [119]1 Kgs. [1 Sam.] 16: 13.

Ode 7

EIRMOS: *We have sinned, we have transgressed, we have done evil in Thy sight; we have not kept or followed Thy commandments. But reject us not utterly, O God of our fathers.*

REFRAIN: *Have mercy on me, O God, have mercy on me.*

I have sinned, I have offended, I have set aside Thy commandments; for in sins have I progressed and to my sores I have added wounds. But in Thy compassion have mercy upon me, O God of our fathers.

The secrets of my heart have I confessed to Thee, my Judge. See my abasement, see my affliction, and attend to my judgement now; and in Thy compassion have mercy upon me, O God of our fathers.

When Saul once lost his father's asses, in searching for them he found himself proclaimed as king. But watch, my soul, lest unknown to thyself thou prefer thine animal appetites to the Kingdom of Christ.[120]

David, the forefather of God, once sinned doubly, pierced with the arrow of adultery and the spear of murder. But thou, my soul, art more gravely sick than he, for worse than any acts are the impulses of thy will.[121]

David once joined sin to sin, adding murder to fornication; yet then he showed at once a twofold repentance. But thou, my soul, hast done worse things than he, yet thou hast not repented before God.[122]

David once composed a hymn, setting forth, as in an ikon, the action he had done; and he condemned it, crying: 'Have mercy upon me, for against Thee only have I sinned, O God of all. Do Thou cleanse me.'[123]

When the Ark was being carried in a cart and the ox stumbled, Uzzah did no more than touch it, but the wrath of God smote him. O my soul, flee from his presumption and respect with reverence the things of God.[124]

Thou hast heard of Absalom, and how he rebelled against nature; thou knowest of the unholy deeds by which he defiled his father David's bed. Yet thou hast followed him in his passionate and sensual desires.[125]

Thy free dignity, O my soul, thou hast subjected to thy body; for thou hast found in the enemy another Ahitophel, and hast agreed to all his counsels. But Christ Himself has brought them to nothing and saved thee from them all.[126]

[120] 1 Kgs. [1 Sam.] 9:3; 10: 1–2.   [121] 2 Kgs. [2 Sam.] 11:2–17.
[122] 2 Kgs. [2 Sam.] 12:13.   [123] Ps. 50:3, 6 ,11.   [124] 2 Kgs.[[2 Sam] 6: 6–7.
[125] 2 Kgs. [2Sam.]16: 21–22.   [126] 2 Kgs. [2 Sam] 16: 23.

Solomon the wonderful, who was full of the grace of wisdom, once did evil in the sight of heaven and turned away from God. Thou hast become like him, my soul, through thine accursed life.[127]

Carried away by sensual passions, he defiled himself. Alas! The lover of wisdom became a lover of harlots and a stranger to God. And thou, my soul, in thy mind hast imitated him through thy shameful desires.[128]

O my soul, thou hast rivalled Rehoboam, who paid no attention to his father's counsellors, and Jeroboam, that evil servant and renegade of old. But flee from their example and cry to God: I have sinned, take pity on me.[129]

Alas, my soul! Thou hast rivalled Ahab in guilt. Thou hast become the dwelling-place of fleshly defilements and a shameful vessel of the passions. But groan from the depths of thy heart, and confess thy sins to God.[130]

Elijah once destroyed with fire twice fifty of Jezebel's servants, and he slew the prophets of shame, as a rebuke to Ahab. But flee from the example of both of them, my soul, and be strong.[131]

Heaven is closed to thee, my soul, and a famine from God has seized thee: for thou hast been disobedient, as Ahab was to the words of Elijah the Tishbite. But imitate the widow of Zarephath, and feed the prophet's soul.[132]

By deliberate choice, my soul, thou hast incurred the guilt of Manasseh, setting up the passions as idols and multiplying abominations. But with fervent heart emulate his repentance and acquire compunction.[133]

I fall before Thee, and as tears I offer Thee my words. I have sinned as the Harlot never sinned, and I have transgressed as no other man on earth. But take pity on Thy creature, O Master, and call me back.[134]

I have discoloured Thine image and broken Thy commandment. All my beauty is destroyed and my lamp is quenched by the passions, O Saviour. But take pity on me, as David sings, and 'restore to me Thy joy.'[135]

Turn back, repent, uncover all that thou hast hidden. Say unto God, to whom all things are known: Thou alone knowest my secrets, O Saviour; 'have mercy on me', as David sings, 'according to Thy mercy.'[136]

My days have vanished as the dream of one awaking: and so, like Hezekiah, I weep upon my bed, that years may be added to my life. But what Isaiah will come to thee, my soul, except the God of all?[137]

---

[127]3 [1] Kgs. 11:1–10.   [128]3 [1] Kgs. 3: 12; 11: 1.   [129]3 [1] Kgs. 11:26–40, 12: 1–33.
[130]3 [1] Kgs 1.6: 30.   [131]4 [2] Kgs. 1: 10–15; 3 Kgs. 18: 40.   [132]3[1] Kgs. 17:1; Lk. 4:25.
[133]4 [2] Kgs. 21; 2 Chron. 33:11–13; the Prayer of Manasseh.   [134]Lk. 7: 37.
[135]Ps. 50: 14.   [136]Ps. 50:3.   [137]Ps. 72:20; 4 Kgs. [2] 20: 1–6; Isa. 38:2.

REFRAIN: *Holy mother Mary, pray to God for us.*

Raising thy cry to the pure Mother of God, thou hast driven back the fury of the passions that violently assailed thee, and put to shame the enemy who sought to make thee stumble. But give thy help in trouble now to me also, thy servant.

REFRAIN: *Holy mother Mary, pray to God for us.*

He whom thou hast loved, O Mother, whom thou hast desired, in whose footsteps thou hast followed: He it was who found thee and gave thee repentance, for He is God compassionate. Pray to Him without ceasing, that we may be delivered from passions and distress.

REFRAIN: *Holy father Andrew, pray to God for us.*

Set me firmly on the rock of faith, O father, through thine intercessions; fence me round with fear of God, O Andrew; grant repentance to me now, I beseech thee, and deliver me from the snare of the enemies that seek my life.

Glory to the Father, and to the Son, and to the Holy Spirit.

O simple and undivided Trinity, one consubstantial Nature: Thou art praised as Light and Lights, one Holy and three Holies. Sing, O my soul, and glorify Life and Lives, the God of all.

Both now and ever, and unto the ages of ages. Amen.

We praise thee, we bless thee, we venerate thee, O Mother of God: for thou hast given birth to One of the undivided Trinity, thy Son and God, and thou hast opened the heavenly places to us on earth.

THE TRIODION
Ode 8 · Tone 8

EIRMOS: *The eternal King of glory, before whom the powers of heaven tremble and the ranks of angels stand in fear, O ye priests praise and ye people exalt above all for ever.*

REFRAIN: *Holy Apostles, pray to God for us.*

As coals of immaterial fire, O apostles, burn up my material passions and kindle within me now a longing for divine love.

Let us honour the well-tuned trumpets of the Word, which have caused the ill-founded walls of the enemy to fall, and have firmly established the ramparts of the knowledge of God.[138]

[138]Josh. 6: 20.

Break in pieces the passionate idols of my soul, as ye brake in pieces the temples and pillars of the enemy, O apostles of the Lord, consecrated temples.[139]

Most holy Theotokos, save us.

O pure Virgin, thou hast contained Him who by nature cannot be contained; thou hast held Him who upholds all things; thou hast given suck to Him who sustains the creation, Christ the Giver of Life.

ANOTHER TRIODION, WITH THE SAME EIRMOS

REFRAIN: *Holy Apostles, pray to God for us.*

O apostles of Christ, with the Spirit as architect ye have built the whole Church, and within it ye bless Christ for ever.

Sounding the trumpets of the dogmas, the apostles have over-thrown all the error of idolatry, exalting Christ above all for ever.

O noble company of the apostles who watch over the world and dwell in heaven, deliver from danger those who ever sing your praises.

Most Holy Trinity, our God, Glory to Thee.

O threefold Sun, all-radiant Sovereignty of God, O Nature one in glory, one in throne: Father all-creating, Son and Spirit of God, I praise Thee for ever.

Most holy Theotokos, save us.

As a throne honoured and most high, let us praise in ceaseless song the Mother of God, O ye peoples, for she alone is both a Mother and a Virgin after childbirth.

THE GREAT CANON
Ode 8 · Tone 6

EIRMOS: *The hosts of heaven give Him glory; before Him tremble cherubim and seraphim; let everything that has breath and all creation praise Him, bless Him, and exalt Him above all for ever.*

REFRAIN: *Have mercy on me, O God, have mercy on me.*

I have sinned, O Saviour, have mercy on me. Awaken my mind and turn me back; accept me in repentance and take pity on me as I cry: against Thee only have I sinned; I have done evil, have mercy on me.

[139]Eph. 2: 20–1.

Riding in the chariot of the virtues, Elijah was lifted up to heaven, high above earthly things. Reflect, my soul, on his ascent.[140]

With the mantle of Elijah, Elisha made the stream of Jordan stand still on either side: but in this grace, my soul, thou hast no share, by reason of thy greed and uncontrolled desires.[141]

Elisha once took up the mantle of Elijah, and received a double portion of grace from the Lord: but in this grace, my soul, thou hast no share, by reason of thy greed and uncontrolled desires.[142]

The Shunammite woman gladly entertained the righteous Prophet: but in thy house, my soul, thou hast not welcomed stranger or traveller; and so thou shalt be cast out weeping from the bridal chamber.[143]

O wretched soul, always thou hast imitated the polluted thoughts of Gehazi. Cast from thee, at least in thine old age, his love of money. Flee from the fire of hell, turn away from thy wickedness.[144]

Thou hast followed Uzziah, my soul, and hast his leprosy in double form; for thy thoughts are wicked, and thine acts unlawful. Leave what thou hast, and hasten to repentance.[145]

O my soul, thou hast heard how the men of Nineveh repented before God in sackcloth and ashes. Yet thou hast not followed them, but art more wicked than all who sinned before the Law and after.[146]

Thou hast heard, my soul, how Jeremiah in the muddy pit cried out with lamentations for the city of Zion and asked to be given tears. Follow his life of lamentation and be saved.[147]

Jonah fled to Tarshish, foreseeing the conversion of the men of Nineveh; for as a prophet he knew the loving-kindness of God, but he was jealous that his prophecy should not be proved false.[148]

My soul, thou hast heard how Daniel stopped the mouths of the wild beasts in the lions' den; and thou knowest how the Children with Azarias quenched through their faith the flames of the fiery furnace.[149]

All the names of the Old Testament have I set before thee, my soul, as an example. Imitate the holy acts of the righteous and flee from the sins of the wicked.

---

[140]4 [2] Kgs. 2: 11.   [141]4 [2] Kgs. 2: 14.   [142]4 [2] Kgs. 2: 9, 13.
[143]4 [2] Kgs. 4: 8; Matt. 22:1–13.   [144]4 [2] Kgs. 5: 21–27.   [145]2 Chron. 26: 19
[146]Jon. 3: 5.   [147]Jer. 45 [38]:6, 9:1.   [148]Jon. 1: 3.   [149]Dan. 6: 16–22; 3: 23–25.

O righteous Judge and Saviour, have mercy on me and deliver me from the fire that threatens me, and from the punishment that I deserve to suffer at the Judgement. Before the end comes, grant me remission through virtue and repentance.

Like the Thief I cry to Thee, 'Remember me'; like Peter I weep bitterly; like the Publican I call out, 'Forgive me, Saviour'; like the Harlot I shed tears. Accept my lamentation, as once Thou hast accepted the entreaties of the woman of Canaan.[150]

O Saviour, heal the putrefaction of my humbled soul, for Thou art the one Physician; apply plaster, and pour in oil and wine—works of repentance, and compunction with tears.[151]

Like the woman of Canaan, I cry to Thee, 'Have mercy on me, Son of David.' Like the woman with an issue of blood, I touch the hem of Thy garment. I weep as Martha and Mary wept for Lazarus.[152]

As precious ointment, O Saviour, I empty on Thine head the alabaster box of my tears. Like the Harlot, I cry out to Thee, seeking mercy: I bring my prayer and ask to receive forgiveness.[153]

No one has sinned against Thee as I have; yet accept even me, compassionate Saviour, for I repent in fear and cry with longing: Against Thee alone have I sinned; I have transgressed, have mercy on me.[154]

Spare the work of Thine own hands, O Saviour, and as shepherd seek the lost sheep that has gone astray. Snatch me from the wolf and make me a nursling in the pasture of Thine own flock.[155]

When Thou sittest upon Thy throne, O merciful Judge, and revealest Thy dread glory, O Christ, what fear there will be then! When the furnace burns with fire, and all shrink back in terror before Thy judgement-seat.[156]

REFRAIN: *Holy mother Mary, pray to God for us.*

The Mother of the Light that never sets illumined thee and freed thee from the darkness of the passions. O Mary, who hast received the grace of the Spirit, give light to those who praise thee with faith.

REFRAIN: *Holy mother Mary, pray to God for us.*

[150]Lk. 23: 42; Matt. 26: 75; Lk. 18: 13; Lk. 7: 37–38; Matt. 15: 22–28.
[151]Lk. 10: 34.   [152]Matt. 15: 22; Mk. 5 :27; Jn. 11: 33.
[153]Matt. 26: 7; Lk. 7: 37–38.   [154]Ps. 50: 6.
[155]Ps. 118: 176; Lk. 15:4; Jn. 10: 11–12.   [156]Dan. 7:9–10; Jn.5:22; Matt. 24: 30.

The holy Zosimas was struck with amazement, O Mother, beholding in thee a wonder truly strange and new. For he saw an angel in the body and was filled with astonishment, praising Christ unto all ages.

REFRAIN: *Holy father Andrew, pray to God for us.*

Since thou hast boldness before the Lord, O Andrew, honoured renown of Crete, I beseech thee, intercede that I may find deliverance from the bonds of iniquity through thy prayers, O teacher, glory of holy monks.

We bless the Lord, Father, Son and Holy Spirit.

Father without beginning, coeternal Son, and loving Comforter, the Spirit of righteousness; Begetter of the Word of God, Word of the Eternal Father, Spirit living and creative: O Trinity in Unity, have mercy on me.

Both now and ever, and unto the ages of ages. Amen.

As from purple silk, O undefiled Virgin, the spiritual robe of Emmanuel, His flesh, was woven in thy womb. Therefore we honour thee as Theotokos in very truth.

We praise, we bless, we worship the Lord, praising and supremely exalting Him unto all ages.

AND AGAIN THE EIRMOS: *The hosts of heaven give Him glory; before Him tremble cherubim and seraphim; let everything that has breath and all creation praise Him, bless Him, and exalt Him above all for ever.*

Here we sing the Magnificat.

THEN THE TRIODION

Ode 9 · Tone 8

EIRMOS: *Saved through thee, pure Virgin, we confess thee to be truly Theotokos, and with the choirs of angels we magnify thee.*

REFRAIN: *Holy Apostles, pray to God for us.*

Ye were revealed, O apostles, as fountains of the water of salvation: bring refreshment to my soul that faints from the thirst of sin.

I am swimming in the deep waters of destruction and have come near to drowning: with Thy right hand, O Lord, save me as Thou hast saved Peter.[157]

---

[157]Matt. 14: 31.

Ye are the salt that gives savor to the teachings of salvation: dry up the rottenness of my mind and dispel the darkness of my ignorance.[158]

Most holy Theotokos, save us.

O Lady, thou hast brought forth our Joy: grant me the spirit of mourning that in the coming Day of Judgement I may be comforted by God.[159]

ANOTHER EIRMOS: *With all generations we magnify thee, mediatrix between heaven and earth. For in thee, O Virgin, the fullness of the Godhead came to dwell bodily.*[160]

REFRAIN: *Holy Apostles, pray to God for us.*

We magnify you in our hymns, O glorious company of the apostles: for ye have been revealed as shining lights of the inhabited earth, driving out error.

O blessed apostles, catching rational fish with the net of the Gospel, bring them always as an offering to Christ.

In your prayers to God remember us, we entreat you, O apostles. May we be delivered from all temptation, for lovingly we sing your praises.

Most Holy Trinity, our God, Glory to Thee.

I sing Thy praises, Unity in three Persons, Father, Son and Spirit, one God, consubstantial Trinity, equal in power and without beginning.

Most holy Theotokos, save us.

With all generations we call thee blessed, O Mother and Virgin: through thee we are delivered from the curse, for thou hast borne the Lord our Joy.

AND THE REST OF THE GREAT CANON

Ode 9 · Tone 6

EIRMOS: *Conception without seed; nativity past understanding, from a Mother who never knew a man; childbearing undefiled. For the birth of God makes both natures new. Therefore, as Bride and Mother of God, with true worship all generations magnify thee.*

REFRAIN: *Have mercy on me, O God, have mercy on me.*

My mind is wounded, my body has grown feeble, my spirit is sick, my speech has lost its power, my life is dead; the end is at the door. What shalt thou do, then, miserable soul, when the Judge comes to examine thy deeds?

[158]Matt. 5: 13.   [159]Matt. 5: 4.   [160]Col. 2: 9.

I have put before thee, my soul, Moses' account of the creation of the world, and after that all the recognized Scriptures that tell thee the story of the righteous and the wicked. But thou, my soul, hast followed the second of these, not the first, and hast sinned against God.

The Law is powerless, the Gospel of no effect, and the whole of Scripture is ignored by thee; the prophets and all the words of the righteous are useless. Thy wounds, my soul, have been multiplied, and there is no physician to heal thee.

I bring thee, O my soul, examples from the New Testament, to lead thee to compunction. Follow the example of the righteous, turn away from the sinful; and through prayers and fasting, through chastity and reverence, win back Christ's mercy.

Christ became man, calling to repentance thieves and harlots. Repent, my soul: the door of the Kingdom is already open, and pharisees and publicans and adulterers pass through it before thee, changing their life.[161]

Christ became a child and shared in my flesh; and willingly He performed all that belongs to my nature, only without sin. He set before thee, my soul, an example and image of His condescension.[162]

Christ saved the Wise Men and called the Shepherds; He revealed as martyrs a multitude of young children; He glorified the Elder and the aged Widow. But thou, my soul, hast not followed their lives and actions. Woe to thee when thou art judged![163]

The Lord fasted forty days in the wilderness, and at the end of them He was hungry, thus showing that He is man. Do not be dismayed, my soul: if the enemy attacks thee, through prayer and fasting drive him away.[164]

Christ was being tempted; the devil tempted Him, showing Him the stones that they might be made bread. He led Him up into a mountain, to see in an instant all the kingdoms of the world. O my soul, look with fear on what happened; watch and pray every hour to God.[165]

The Dove who loved the wilderness, the Lamp of Christ, the voice of one crying aloud, was heard preaching repentance; but Herod sinned with Herodias. O my soul, see that thou art not trapped in the snares of the transgressors, but embrace repentance.[166]

---

[161]Matt 9: 13; 21: 31; Lk. 15: 1.   [162]Heb. 4: 15.

[163]Matt. 2: 12; Lk. 2: 9–12; Matt. 2: 16; Lk. 2: 25–38.   [164]Matt. 4: 2; 17: 21.

[165]Matt. 4: 3–9; 26: 41.   [166]Ps. 54:7, 123:7; Isa. 40:3; Jn 5:35; Mk. 1: 3; Matt. 3:2–3, 14: 3.

The Forerunner of grace went to dwell in the wilderness, and Judaea and all Samaria ran to hear him; they confessed their sins and were baptized eagerly. But thou, my soul, hast not imitated them.[167]

Marriage is honourable, and the marriage-bed undefiled. For on both Christ has given His blessing, eating in the flesh at the wedding in Cana, turning water into wine and revealing His first miracle, to bring thee, my soul, to a change of life.[168]

Christ gave strength to the paralysed man, and he took up his bed; He raised from the dead the young man, the son of the widow, and the centurion's servant; He appeared to the woman of Samaria, and spoke to thee, my soul, of worship in spirit.[169]

By the touch of the hem of His garment, the Lord healed the woman with an issue of blood; He cleansed lepers and gave sight to the blind and made the lame walk upright; He cured by His word the deaf and the dumb and the woman bowed to the ground, to bring thee, wretched soul, to salvation.[170]

Healing sickness, Christ the Word preached the good tidings to the poor. He cured the crippled, ate with publicans, and conversed with sinners. With the touch of His hand, He brought back the departed soul of Jairus' daughter.[171]

The Publican was saved and the Harlot turned to chastity, but the Pharisee with his boasting was condemned. For the first cried, 'Be merciful', and the second, 'Have mercy on me'; but the third said, boasting, 'I thank Thee, O God', and the other words of madness.[172]

Zacchaeus was a publican, yet he was saved; but Simon the Pharisee went astray, while the Harlot received remission and release from Him who has the power to forgive sins. O my soul, gain His mercy.[173]

O wretched soul, thou hast not acted like the Harlot, who took the alabaster box of precious ointment, and anointed with tears and wiped with her hair the feet of the Lord. And He tore in pieces the record of her previous sins.[174]

Thou knowest, O my soul, how the cities were cursed to which Christ preached the Gospel. Fear their example, lest thou suffer the same punishment. For the Master likened them to Sodom and condemned them to hell.[175]

---

[167]Matt. 3: 5–6.   [168]Heb. 13. 4; Jn. 2: 1–11.

[169]Matt. 9: 2–7; Lk. 7: 14; Matt. 8: 6–13; Jn. 4: 26; Josh. 4: 24.

[170]Matt. 9: 20–22; 10: 8; 11: 5; Lk. 13: 11–13.

[171]Matt. 11:5; Mk. 5: 41–42; Lk. 4:17–19, 5:27–30.   [172]Lk. 7: 36–50; 18: 9–13.

[173]Lk. 19: 1–10; 7: 36–50..   [174]Lk. 7: 37–38; Col. 2: 14.   [175]Lk. 10: 13–15.

Be not overcome by despair, O my soul; for thou hast heard of the faith of the woman of Canaan, and how through it her daughter was healed by the word of God. Cry out from the depth of thy heart, 'Save me also, Son of David', as she once cried to Christ.[176]

O Son of David, with Thy word Thou hast healed the possessed: take pity on me, save me and have mercy. Let me hear Thy compassionate voice speak to me as to the thief: 'Verily, I say unto thee, thou shalt be with Me in Paradise, when I come in My glory.'[177]

A thief accused Thee, a thief confessed Thy Godhead: for both were hanging with Thee on the Cross. Open to me also, O Lord of many mercies, the door of Thy glorious Kingdom, as once it was opened to Thy thief who acknowledged Thee with faith as God.[178]

The creation was in anguish, seeing Thee crucified. Mountains and rocks were split from fear, the earth quaked, and hell was despoiled; the light grew dark in daytime, beholding Thee, O Jesus, nailed in the flesh.[179]

Do not demand from me worthy fruits of repentance, for my strength has failed within me. Give me an ever-contrite heart and poverty of spirit, that I may offer these to Thee as an acceptable sacrifice, O only Saviour.[180]

O my Judge who dost know me, when Thou comest again with the angels to judge the whole world, look upon me then with Thine eye of mercy, and spare me; take pity on me, Jesus, for I have sinned more than any other man.

REFRAIN: *Holy mother Mary, pray to God for us.*

By thy strange way of life thou hast struck all with wonder, both the hosts of angels and the gatherings of mortal men; for thou hast surpassed nature and lived as though no longer in the body. Like a bodiless angel thou hast walked upon the Jordan with thy feet, O Mary, and crossed over it.

REFRAIN: *Holy mother Mary, pray to God for us.*

O holy Mother, call down the gracious mercy of the Creator upon us who sing thy praises, that we may be set free from the sufferings and afflictions that assail us; so without ceasing, delivered from temptations, we shall magnify the Lord who has glorified thee.

REFRAIN: *Holy father Andrew, pray to God for us.*

---

[176]Matt. 15: 22.   [177]Lk. 9: 38–42; 23: 43.
[178]Lk. 23: 32, 39–43.   [179]Matt. 27: 51–53; Lk. 23: 44–45.   [180]Matt. 3: 8; 5: 3; Ps. 50: 17.

Venerable Andrew, father thrice-blessed, shepherd of Crete, cease not to offer prayer for us who sing thy praises; that we may be delivered from all danger and distress, from corruption and innumerable sins, who honour thy memory with faith.

Glory to the Father, and to the Son, and to the Holy Spirit.

Trinity one in Essence, Unity in three Persons, we sing Thy praises: we glorify the Father, we magnify the Son, we worship the Spirit, truly one God by nature, Life and Lives, Kingdom without end.

Both now and ever, and unto the ages of ages. Amen.

Watch over thy City, all-pure Mother of God. For by thee she reigns in faith, by thee she is made strong; by thee she is victorious, putting to flight every temptation, despoiling the enemy and ruling her subjects.

AND AGAIN THE EIRMOS: *Conception without seed; nativity past understanding, from a Mother who never knew a man; childbearing undefiled. For the birth of God makes both natures new. Therefore, as Bride and Mother of God, with true worship all generations magnify thee.*

LITTLE LITANY: Again and again in peace . . .

EXCLAMATION: For all the hosts of heaven praise Thee . . .

CHOIR: Amen.

Then the Photogogikon or Lucern of the Trinity, tone 8:

O Thou Who art the Light, enlighten . . .

The Praises and Doxology are read, not sung.

The Life

of Our

Holy Mother

MARY of EGYPT

*I*t is good to hide the secret of a king, but it is glorious to reveal and preach the works of God.[1] So said the Archangel Raphael to Tobit when he performed the wonderful healing of his blindness. Actually, not to keep the secret of a king is perilous and a terrible risk, but to be silent about the works of God is a great loss for the soul. And I (says St. Sophronius), in writing the life of St. Mary of Egypt, am afraid to hide the works of God by silence. Remembering the misfortune threatened to the servant who hid his God-given talent in the earth.[2] I am bound to pass on the holy account that has reached me. And let no one think (continues St. Sophronius) that I have had the audacity to write untruth or doubt this great marvel—may I never lie about holy things! If there do happen to be people who, after reading this record, do not believe it, may the Lord have mercy on them because, reflecting on the weakness of human nature, they consider impossible these wonderful things accomplished by holy people. But now we must begin to tell this most amazing story, which has taken place in our generation.

There was a certain elder in one of the monasteries of Palestine, a priest of holy life and speech, who from childhood had been brought up in monastic ways and customs. This elder's name was Zosimas. He had been through the whole course of the ascetic life and in everything he adhered to the rule once given to him by his tutors as regard spiritual labours. He had also added a good deal himself whilst labouring to subject his flesh to the will of the spirit. And he had not failed in his aim. He was so renowned for his spiritual life that many came to him from neighbouring monasteries and some even from afar. While doing all this, he never ceased to study the Divine Scriptures. Whether resting, standing, working or eating food (if the scraps he nibbled could be called food), he incessantly and constantly had a single aim: always to sing of God, and to practice the teaching of the Divine Scriptures. Zosimas used to relate how, as soon as he was taken from his mother's breast, he was handed over to the monastery where he went through his training as an ascetic till he reached the age of 53. After that, he began to be tormented with the thought that he was perfect in everything and needed no instruction from anyone, saying to himself mentally, "Is there a monk on earth who can be of use to me and show me a kind of asceticism that I have not accomplished? Is there a man to be found in the desert who has surpassed me?"

Thus thought the elder, when suddenly an angel appeared to him and said:

[1]Tobit 12:7.
[2]Matt. 25:18–25.

"Zosimas, valiantly have you struggled, as far as this is within the power of man, valiantly have you gone through the ascetic course. But there is no man who has attained perfection. Before you lie unknown struggles greater than those you have accomplished. That you may know how many other ways lead to salvation, leave your native land like the renowned Patriarch Abraham and go to the monastery by the River Jordan."

Zosimas did as he was told. He left the monastery in which he had lived from childhood, and went to the River Jordan. At last he reached the community to which God had sent him. Having knocked at the door of the monastery, he told the monk who was the porter who he was; and the porter told the abbot. On being admitted to the abbot's presence, Zosimas made the usual monastic prostration and prayer. Seeing that he was a monk the abbot asked:

"Where do you come from, brother, and why have you come to us poor old men?"

Zosimas replied:

"There is no need to speak about where I have come from, but I have come, father, seeking spiritual profit, for I have heard great things about your skill in leading souls to God."

"Brother," the abbot said to him, "Only God can heal the infirmity of the soul. May He teach you and us His divine ways and guide us. But as it is the love of Christ that has moved you to visit us poor old men, then stay with us, if that is why you have come. May the Good Shepherd Who laid down His life for our salvation fill us all with the grace of the Holy Spirit."

After this, Zosimas bowed to the abbot, asked for his prayers and blessing, and stayed in the monastery. There he saw elders proficient both in action and the contemplation of God, aflame in spirit, working for the Lord. They sang incessantly, they stood in prayer all night, work was ever in their hands and psalms on their lips. Never an idle word was heard among them, they knew nothing about acquiring temporal goods or of the cares of life. But they had one desire—to become in body like corpses. Their constant food was the Word of God, and they sustained their bodies on bread and water, as much as their love for God allowed them. Seeing this, Zosimas was greatly edified and prepared for the struggle that lay before him.

Many days passed and the time drew near when all Christians fast and prepare themselves to worship the Divine Passion and Resurrection of Christ. The monastery gates were kept always locked and only opened when one of the community was sent out on some errand. It was a desert place, not only unvisited by people of the world but even unknown to them.

There was a rule in that monastery which was the reason why God brought Zosimas there. At the beginning of the Great Fast[3] the priest celebrated the holy Liturgy and all partook of the holy Body and Blood of Christ. After the Liturgy they went to the refectory and would eat a little lenten food.

Then all gathered in church, and after praying earnestly with prostrations, the elders kissed one another and asked forgiveness. And each made a prostration to the abbot and asked his blessing and prayers for the struggle that lay before them. After this, the gates of the monastery were thrown open, and singing, *The Lord is my light and my Saviour; whom shall I fear? The Lord is the defender of my life; of whom shall I be afraid?*[4] and the rest of that psalm, all went out into the desert and crossed the River Jordan. Only one or two brothers were left in the monastery, not to guard the property (for there was nothing to rob), but so as not to leave the church without Divine Service. Each took with him as much as he could or wanted in the way of food, according to the needs of his body: one would take a little bread, another some figs, another dates or wheat soaked in water. And some took nothing but their own body covered with rags and fed when nature forced them to it on the plants that grew in the desert.

After crossing the Jordan, they all scattered far and wide in different directions. And this was the rule of life they had, and which they all observed—neither to talk to one another, nor to know how each one lived and fasted. If they did happen to catch sight of one another, they went to another part of the country, living alone and always singing to God, and at a definite time eating a very small quantity of food. In this way they spent the whole of the fast and used to return to the monastery a week before the Resurrection of Christ, on Palm Sunday. Each one returned having his own conscience as the witness of his labour, and no one asked another how he had spent his time in the desert. Such were rules of the monastery. Everyone of them whilst in the desert struggled with himself before the Judge of the struggle—God—not seeking to please men and fast before the eyes of all. For what is done for the sake of men, to win praise and honour, is not only useless to the one who does it but sometimes the cause of great punishment.

Zosimas did the same as all. And he went far, far into the desert with a secret hope of finding some father who might be living there and who might be able to satisfy his thirst and longing. And he wandered on tireless, as if hurrying on to some definite place. He had already walked for 20 days and when the 6th hour came he stopped and, turning to the East, he began to sing the Sixth Hour and

[3]on "Forgiveness Sunday."
[4]Ps. 26:1.

recite the customary prayers. He used to break his journey thus at fixed hours of the day to rest a little, to chant psalms standing and to pray on bent knees.

And as he sang thus without turning his eyes from the heavens, he suddenly saw to the right of the hillock on which he stood the semblance of a human body. At first he was confused thinking he beheld a vision of the devil, and even started with fear. But, having guarded himself with the sign of the Cross and banished all fear, he turned his gaze in that direction and in truth saw some form gliding southwards. It was naked, the skin dark as if burned up by heat of the sun; the hair on its head was white as a fleece, and not long, falling just below its neck. Zosimas was so overjoyed at beholding a human form that he ran after it in pursuit, but the form fled from him. He followed. At length, when he was near enough to be heard, he shouted:

"Why do you run away from an old man and a sinner? Slave of the True God, wait for me, whoever you are, in God's name I tell you, for the love of God for Whose sake you are living in this desert."

"Forgive me for God's sake, but I cannot turn towards you and show you my face, Abba. Zosimas. For I am a woman and naked as you see with the uncovered shame of my body. But if you would like to fulfil one wish of a sinful woman, throw me your cloak so that I can cover my body and can turn to you and ask for your blessing."

Here terror seized Zosimas, for he heard that she called him by name. But he realized that she could not have done so without knowing anything of him if she had not had the power of spiritual insight.

He at once did as he was asked. He took off his old, tattered cloak and threw it to her, turning away as he did so. She picked it up and was able to cover at least a part of her body. Then she turned to Zosimas and said:

"Why did you wish, Abba Zosimas, to see a sinful woman? What do you wish to hear or learn from me, you who have not shrunk from such great struggles?"

Zosimas threw himself on the ground and asked for her blessing. She likewise bowed down before him. And thus they lay on the ground prostrate asking for each other's blessing. And one word alone could be heard from both: "Bless me!" After a long while the woman said to Zosimas:

"Abba Zosimas, it is you who must give blessings and pray. You are dignified by the order of priesthood and for many years you have been standing before the holy altar and offering the sacrifice of the Divine Mysteries."

This flung Zosimas into even greater terror. At length with tears he said to her:

"O mother, filled with the Spirit, by your mode of life it is evident that you live with God and have died to the world. The Grace granted to you is apparent—for you have called me by name and recognized that I am a priest, though you have never seen me before. Grace is recognized not by one's orders, but by gifts of the Spirit, so give me your belssing for God's sake, for I need your prayers."

Then giving way before the wish of the elder the woman said:

"Blessed is God Who cares for the salvation of men and their souls."

Zosimas answered:

"Amen."

And both rose to their feet. Then the woman asked the elder:

"Why have you come, man of God, to me who am so sinful? Why do you wish to see a woman naked and devoid of every virtue? Though I know one thing—the Grace of the Holy Spirit has brought you to render me a service in time. Tell me, father, how are the Christian peoples living? And the kings? How is the Church guided?"

Zosimas said:

"By your holy prayers, mother, Christ has granted lasting peace to all. But fulfill the unworthy petition of an old man and pray for the whole world and for me who am a sinner, so that my wanderings in the desert may not be fruitless."

She answered:

"You who are a priest, Abba Zosimas, it is you who must pray for me and for all—for this is your calling. But as we must all be obedient, I will gladly do what you ask."

And with these words she turned to the East, and raising her eyes to heaven and stretching out her hands, she began to pray in a whisper. One could not hear separate words, so that Zosimas could not understand anything that she said in her prayers. Meanwhile he stood, according to his own word, all in a flutter, looking at the ground without saying a word. And he swore, calling God to witness, that when at length he thought that her prayer was very long, he took his eyes off the ground and saw that she was raised about a forearm's distance from the ground and stood praying in the air. When he saw this, even greater terror seized him and he fell on the ground weeping and repeating many times, "Lord, have mercy."

And whilst lying prostrate on the ground he was tempted by a thought: Is it not a spirit, and perhaps her prayer is hypocrisy? But at the very same moment the woman turned round, raised the elder from the ground and said:

"Why do thoughts confuse you, Abba, and tempt you about me, as if I were a spirit and a dissembler in prayer? Know, holy father, that I am only a sinful woman, though I am guarded by Holy Baptism. And I am no spirit but earth and ashes, and flesh alone."

And with these words she guarded herself with the sign of the Cross on her forehead, eyes, mouth and breast, saying:

"May God defend us from the evil one and from his designs, for fierce is his struggle against us."

Hearing and seeing this, the elder fell to the ground and, embracing her feet, he said with tears:

"I beg you, by the Name of Christ our God, Who was born of a Virgin, for Whose sake you have stripped yourself, for Whose sake you have exhausted your flesh, do not hide from your slave, who you are and whence and how you came into this desert. Tell me everything so that the marvellous works of God may become known. A hidden wisdom and a secret treasure—what profit is there in them? Tell me all, I implore you. For not out of vanity or for self-display will you speak but to reveal the truth to me, an unworthy sinner. I believe in God, for Whom you live and Whom you serve. I believe that He led me into this desert so as to show me His ways in regard to you. It is not in our power to resist the plans of God. If it were not the will of God that you and your life should be known, He would not have allowed me to see you and would not have strengthened me to undertake this journey, one like me who never before dared to leave his cell."

Much more said Abba Zosimas. But the woman raised him and said:

"I am ashamed, Abba, to speak to you of my disgraceful life, forgive me for God's sake! But as you have already seen my naked body I shall likewise lay bare before you my work, so that you may know with what shame and obscenity my soul is filled. I was not running away out of vanity, as you thought, for what have I to be proud of—I who was the chosen vessel of the devil? But when I start my story you will run from me, as from a snake, for your ears will not be able to bear the vileness of my actions. But I shall tell you all without hiding anything, only imploring you first of all to pray incessantly for me, so that I may find mercy on the day of Judgment."

The elder wept and the woman began her story.

"My native land, holy father, was Egypt. Already during the lifetime of my parents, when I was twelve years old, I renounced their love and and went to Alexandria. I am ashamed to recall how there I at first ruined my maidenhood and then unrestrainedly and insatiably gave myself up to sensuality. It is more becoming to speak of this briefly, so that you may just know my passion and my lechery. For about seventeen years, forgive me, I lived like that. I was like a fire of public debauch. And it was not for the sake of gain—here I speak the pure truth.

Often when they wished to pay me, I refused the money. I acted in this way so as to make as many men as possible try to obtain me, doing free of charge what gave me pleasure. Do not think that I was rich and that was the reason why I did not take money. I lived by begging, often by spinning flax, but I had an insatiable desire and an irrepressible passion for lying in filth. This was life to me. Every kind of abuse of nature I regarded as life.

"That is how I lived. Then one summer I saw a large crowd of Lybians and Egyptians running towards the sea. I asked one of them, 'Where are these men hurrying to?" He replied, 'They are all going to Jerusalem for the Exaltation of the Precious and Lifegiving Cross, which takes place in a few days.' I said to him, 'Will they take me with them if I wish to go?' 'No one will hinder you if you have money to pay for the journey and for food.' And I said to him, 'To tell you truth, I have no money, neither have I food. But I shall go with them and shall go aboard. And they shall feed me, whether they want to or not. I have a body—they shall take it instead of pay for the journey.' I was suddenly filled with a desire to go, Abba, to have more lovers who could satisfy my passion. I told you, Abba Zosimas, not to force me to tell you of my disgrace. God is my witness, I am afraid of defiling you and the very air with my words."

Zosimas, weeping, replied to her:

"Speak on for God's sake, mother, speak and do not break the thread of such an edifying tale."

And, resuming her story, she went on:

"That youth, on hearing my shameless words, laughed and went off. While I, throwing away my spinning wheel, ran off towards the sea in the direction which everyone seemed to be taking. And, seeing some young men standing on the shore, about ten or more of them, full of vigour and alert in their movements, I decided that they would do for my purpose (it seemed that some of them were waiting for more travellers whilst others had gone ashore). Shamelessly, as usual, I mixed with the crowd, saying, 'Take me with you to the place you are going to; you will not find me superfluous.' I also added a few more words calling forth general laughter. Seeing my readiness to be shameless, they readily took me aboard the boat. Those who were expected came also, and we set sail at once.

"How shall I relate to you what happened after this? Whose tongue can tell, whose ears can take in all that took place on the boat during that voyage! And to all this I frequently forced those miserable youths even against their own will. There is no mentionable or unmentionable depravity of which I was not their teacher. I am amazed, Abba, how the sea stood our licentiousness, how the earth did not open its jaws, and how it was that hell did not swallow me alive, when I had entangled in my net so many souls. But I think God was seeking my repentance. For He does not desire the death of a sinner but magnanimously awaits his return to Him. At last we arrived in Jerusalem. I spent the days before the festival in the town, living the same kind of life, perhaps even worse. I was not content with the youths I had seduced at sea and who had helped me to get to Jerusalem; many others—citizens of the town and foreigners—I also seduced.

"The holy day of the Exaltation of the Cross dawned while I was still flying about—hunting for youths. At daybreak I saw that everyone was hurrying to the church, so I ran with the rest. When the hour for the holy elevation approached, I was trying to make my way in with the crowd which was struggling to get through the church doors. I had at last squeezed through with great difficulty almost to the entrance of the temple, from which the lifegiving Tree of the Cross was being shown to the people. But when I trod on the doorstep which everyone passed, I was stopped by some force which prevented my entering. Meanwhile I was brushed aside by the crowd and found myself standing alone in the porch. Thinking that this had happened because of my woman's weakness, I again began to work my way into the crowd, trying to elbow myself forward. But in vain I struggled. Again my feet trod on the doorstep over which others were entering the church without encountering any obstacle. I alone seemed to remain unaccepted by the church. It was as if there was a detachment of soldiers standing there to oppose my entrance. Once again I was excluded by the same mighty force and again I stood in the porch.

"Having repeated my attempt three or four times, at last I felt exhausted and had no more strength to push and to be pushed, so I went aside and stood in a corner of the porch. And only then with great difficulty it began to dawn on me, and I began to understand the reason why I was prevented from being admitted to see the life-giving Cross. The word of salvation gently touched the eyes of my heart and revealed to me that it was my unclean life which barred the entrance to me. I began to weep and lament and beat my breast, and to sigh from the depths of my heart. And so I stood weeping when I saw above me the ikon of the most holy Mother of God. And turning to her my bodily and spiritual eyes I said:

"'O Lady, Mother of God, who gave birth in the flesh to God the Word, I know, O how well I know, that it is no honour or praise to thee when one so impure and depraved as I look up to thy ikon, O Ever-Virgin, who didst keep thy body and soul in purity. Rightly do I inspire hatred and disgust before thy virginal purity. But I have heard that God Who was born of thee became man on purpose to call sinners to repentance. Then help me, for I have no other help. Order the entrance of the church to be opened to me. Allow me to see the venerable Tree on which He Who was born of thee suffered in the flesh and on which He shed His holy Blood for the redemption of sinners and for me, unworthy as I am. Be my faithful witness before thy Son that I will never again defile my body by the impurity of fornication, but as soon as I have seen the Tree of the Cross I will renounce the world and its temptations and will go wherever thou wilt lead me.'

"Thus I spoke and as if acquiring some hope in firm faith, and feeling some confidence in the mercy of the Mother of God, I left the place where I stood praying. And I went again and mingled with the crowd that was pushing its way into the temple. And now no one seemed to thwart me, no one hindered my entering the church. I was possessed with trembling, and was almost in delirium. Having got as far as the doors which I could not reach before—as if the same force which had hindered me cleared the way for me—I now entered without difficulty and found myself within the holy place. And so it was I saw the lifegiving Cross. I saw too the Mysteries of God and how the Lord accepts repentance. Throwing myself on the ground, I worshipped that holy earth and kissed it with trembling. Then I came out of the church and went to her who had promised to be my security, to the place where I had sealed my vow. And bending my knees before the Virgin Mother of God, I addressed to her such words as these:

"'O loving Lady, thou hast shown me thy great love for all men. Glory to God Who receives the repentance of sinners through thee. What more can I recollect or say, I who am so sinful? It is time for me, O Lady, to fulfil my vow, according to thy witness. Now lead me by the hand along the path of repentance!' And at these words I heard a voice from on high:

"'If you cross the Jordan you will find glorious rest.'

"Hearing this voice and having faith that it was for me, I cried to the Mother of God:

"'O Lady, Lady, do not forsake me!'

"With these words I left the porch of the church and set off on my journey. As I was leaving the church a stranger glanced at me and gave me three coins, saying:

"'Sister, take these.'

"And, taking the money, I bought three loaves and took them with me on my journey, as a blessed gift. I asked the person who sold the bread: 'Which is the way to the Jordan?' I was directed to the city gate which led that way. Running on I passed the gates and still weeping went on my journey. Those I met I asked the way, and after walking for the rest of that day (I think it was nine o'clock when I saw the Cross) I at length reached at sunset the Church of St. John the

Baptist which stood on the banks of the Jordan. After praying in the temple, I went down to the Jordan and rinsed my face and hands in its holy waters. I partook of the holy and life-giving Mysteries in the Church of the Forerunner and ate half of one of my loaves. Then, after drinking some water from Jordan, I lay down and passed the night on the ground. In the morning I found a small boat and crossed to the opposite bank. I again prayed to Our Lady to lead me whither she wished. Then I found myself in this desert and since then up to this very day I am estranged from all, keeping away from people and running away from everyone. And I live here clinging to my God Who saves all who turn to Him from faintheartedness and storms."

Zosimas asked her:

"How many years have gone by since you began to live in this desert?"

She replied:

"Forty-seven years have already gone by, I think, since I left the holy city."

Zosimas asked:

"But what food do you find?"

The woman said:

"I had two and a half loaves when I crossed the Jordan Soon they dried up and become hard as rock. Eating a little I gradually finished them after a few years."

Zosimas asked.

"Can it be that without getting ill you have lived so many years thus, without suffering in any way from such a complete change?"

The woman answered:

"You remind me, Zosimas, of what I dare not speak of. For when I recall all the dangers which I overcame, and all the violent thoughts which confused me, I am again afraid that they will take possession of me."

Zosimas said:

"Do not hide from me anything; speak to me without concealing anything."

And she said to him: "Believe me, Abba, seventeen years I passed in this desert fighting wild beasts—mad desires and passions. When I was about to partake of food, I used to begin to regret the meat and fish of which I had so much in Egypt. I regretted also not having wine which I loved so much. For I drank a lot of wine when I lived in the world, while here I had not even water. I used to burn and succumb with thirst. The mad desire for profligate songs also entered me and confused me greatly, edging me on to sing satanic songs which I had learned once. But when such desires entered me I struck myself on the breast and reminded myself of the vow which I had made, when going into the desert. In my thoughts I returned to the ikon of the Mother of God which had received me and to her I cried in prayer. I implored her to chase away the thoughts to which my miserable soul was succumbing. And after weeping for long and beating my breast I used to see light at last which seemed to shine on me from everywhere. And after the violent storm, lasting calm descended.

"And how can I tell you about the thoughts which urged me on to fornication, how can I express them to you, Abba? A fire was kindled in my miserable heart which seemed to burn me up completely and to awake in me a thirst for embraces. As soon as this craving came to me, I flung myself on the earth and watered it with my tears, as if I saw before me my witness, who had appeared to me in my disobedience and who seemed to threaten punishment for the crime. And I did not rise from the ground (sometimes I lay thus prostrate for a day and a night) until a calm and sweet light descended and enlightened me and chased away the thoughts that possessed me. But always I turned the eyes of my mind to my Protectress, asking her to extend help to one who was sinking fast in the waves of the desert. And I always had her as my Helper and the Accepter of my repentance. And thus I lived for seventeen years amid constant dangers. And since then even till now the Mother of God helps me in everything and leads me as it were by the hand."

Zosimas asked:

"Can it be that you did not need food and clothing?"

She answered:

"After finishing the loaves I had, of which I spoke, for seventeen years I have fed on herbs and all that can be found in the desert. The clothes I had when I crossed the Jordan became torn and worn out. I suffered greatly from the cold and greatly from the extreme heat: at times the sun burned me up and at other times I shivered from the frost, and frequently falling to the ground I lay without breath and without motion. I struggled with many afflictions and with terrible temptations. But from that time till now the power of God in numerous ways has guarded my sinful soul and my humble body. When I only reflect on the evils from which Our Lord has delivered me I have imperishable food for hope of salvation. I am fed and clothed by the all-powerful Word of God, the Lord of all. For it is not by bread alone that man lives. And those who have stripped off the rags of sin have no refuge, hiding themselves in the clefts of the rocks."[5]

Hearing that she cited words Scripture, from Moses and Job, Zosimas asked her:

"And so you have read the psalms and other books?"

She smiled at this and said to the elder:

[5]Job 24; Heb. 11:38.

"Believe me, I have not seen a human face ever since I crossed the Jordan, except yours today. I have not seen a beast or a living being ever since I came into the desert. I never learned from books. I have never even heard anyone who sang and read from them. But the Word of God which is alive and active, by itself teaches a man knowledge. And so this is the end of my tale. But, as I asked you in the beginning, so even now I implore you for the sake of the Incarnate Word of God, to pray to the Lord for me who am such a sinner."

Thus concluding her tale she bowed down before him. And with tears the elder exclaimed:

"Blessed is God Who creates the great and wondrous, the glorious and marvellous without end. Blessed is God Who has shown me how He rewards those who fear Him. Truly, O Lord, Thou dost not forsake those who seek Thee!"

And the woman, not allowing the elder to bow down before her, said:

"I beg you, holy father, for the sake of Jesus Christ our God and Saviour, tell no one what you have heard, until God delivers me of this earth. And now depart in peace and again next year you shall see me, and I you, if God will preserve us in His great mercy. But for God's sake do as I ask you: Next year during Lent do not cross the Jordan, as is your custom in the monastery."

Zosimas was amazed to hear that she knew the rules of the monastery and could only say:

"Glory to God Who bestows great gifts on those who love Him."

She continued:

"Remain, Abba, in the monastery. And even if you wish to depart, you will not be able to do so. And at sunset of the holy day of the Last Supper, put some of the lifegiving Body and Blood of Christ into a holy vessel worthy to hold such Mysteries for me, and bring it. And wait for me on the banks of the Jordan adjoining the inhabited parts of the land, so that I can come and partake of the lifegiving Gifts. For, since the time I communicated in the temple of the Forerunner before crossing the Jordan even to this day I have not approached the Holy Mysteries. And I thirst for them with irrepressible love and longing. And therefore I ask and implore you to grant me my wish, bring me the lifegiving Mysteries at the very hour when Our Lord made His disciples partake of His Divine Supper. Tell John the Abbot of the monastery where you live: Look to yourself and to your brothers, for there is much that needs correction. Only do not say this now, but when God guides you. Pray for me!"

With these words she vanished in the depths of the desert. And Zosimas, falling down on his knees and bowing down to the ground on which she had stood, sent up glory and thanks to God. And, after wandering through the desert, he returned to the monastery on the day all the brothers returned.

For the whole year he kept silent, not daring to tell anyone of what he had seen. But in his soul he prayed to God to give him another chance of seeing the ascetic's dear face. And when at length the first Sunday of the Great Fast came, all went out into the desert with the customary prayers and the singing of psalms. Only Zosimas was held back by illness—he lay in a fever. And then he remembered what the saint had said to him: "And even if you wish to depart, you will not be able to do so."

Many days passed and at last recovering from his illness he remained in the monastery. And when again the monks returned and the day of the Last Supper dawned, he did as he had been ordered. And placing some of the most pure Body and Blood into a small chalice and putting some figs and dates and lentils soaked in water into a small basket, he departed for the desert and reached the banks of the Jordan and sat down to wait for the saint. He waited for a long while and then began to doubt. Then raising his eyes to heaven, he began to pray:

"Grant me, O Lord, to behold that which Thou hast allowed me to behold once. Do not let me depart in vain, bearing the burden of my sins."

And then another thought struck him:

"And what if she does come? There is no boat; how will she cross the Jordan to come to me who am so unworthy?"

And as he was pondering thus he saw the holy woman appear and stand on the other side of the river. Zosimas got up rejoicing and glorifying and thanking God. And again the thought came to him that she could not cross the Jordan. Then he saw that she made the sign of the Cross over the waters of the Jordan (and the night was a moonlight one, as he related afterwards) and then she at once stepped on to the waters and began moving across the surface towards him. And when he wanted to prostrate himself, she cried to him while still walking on the water:

"What are you doing, Abba, you are a priest and carrying the Divine Gifts!"

He obeyed her and on reaching the shore she said to the elder:

"Bless, father, bless me!"

He answered her trembling, for a state of confusion had overcome him at the sight of the miracle:

"Truly God did not lie when He promised that when we purify ourselves we shall be like Him. Glory to Thee, Christ our God, Who has shown me through this Thy slave how far away I stand from perfection."

Here the woman asked him to say the Creed and Our Father He began, she finished the prayer and according to the custom of that time gave him the kiss of peace on the lips. Having partaken of the Holy Mysteries, she raised her hands to heaven and sighed with tears in her eyes, exclaiming:

"Now lettest Thou Thy servant depart in peace, O Lord, according to Thy word; for my eyes have seen Thy salvation."

Then she said to the elder:

"Forgive me, Abba, for asking you, but fulfil another wish of mine. Go now to the monastery and let God's grace guard you. And next year come again to the same place where I first met you. Come for God's sake, for you shall again see me, for such is the will of God."

He said to her:

"From this day on I would like to follow you and always see your holy face. But now fulfil the one and only wish of an old man and take a little of the food I have brought for you."

And he showed her the basket, while she just touched the lentils with the tips of her fingers, and taking three grains said that the Holy Spirit guards the substance of the soul unpolluted. Then she said:

"Pray, for God's sake pray for me and remember a miserable wretch."

Touching the saint's feet and asking for her prayers for the Church, the kingdom and himself, he let her depart with tears, while he went off sighing and sorrowful, for he could not hope to vanquish the invincible. Meanwhile she again made the sign of the Cross over the Jordan, and stepped on to the waters and crossed over as before. And the elder returned filled with joy and terror, accusing himself of not having asked the saint her name. But he decided to do so next year.

And when another year had passed, he again went into the desert. He reached the same spot but could see no sign of anyone. So raising his eyes to heaven as before, he prayed:

"Show me, O Lord, Thy pure treasure, which Thou hast concealed in the desert. Show me, I pray Thee, Thy angel in the flesh, of which the world is not worthy."

Then on the opposite bank of the river, her face turned towards the rising sun, he saw the saint lying dead Her hands were crossed according to custom and her face was turned to the East. Running up he shed tears over the saint's feet and kissed them, not daring to touch anything else.

For a long time he wept. Then reciting the appointed psalms, he said the burial prayers and thought to himself: "Must I bury the body of a saint? Or will this be contrary to her wishes?" And then he saw words traced on the ground by her head:

"Abba Zosimas, bury on this spot the body of humble Mary. Return to dust that which is dust and pray to the Lord for me, who departed in the month of Fermoutin of Egypt, called April by the Romans, on the first day, on the very night of our Lord's Passion, after having partaken of the Divine Mysteries."[6]

Reading this the elder was glad to know the saint's name. He understood too that as soon as she had partaken of the Divine Mysteries on the shore of the Jordan she was at once transported to the place where she died. The distance which Zosimas had taken twenty days to cover, Mary had evidently traversed in an hour and had at once surrendered her soul to God.

Then Zosimas thought: "It is time to do as she wished. But how am I to dig a grave with nothing in my hands?"

And then he saw nearby a small piece of wood left by some traveller in the desert. Picking it up he began to dig the ground. But the earth was hard and dry and did not yield to the efforts of the elder. He grew tired and covered with sweat. He sighed from the depths of his soul and lifting up his eyes he saw a big lion standing close to the saint's body and licking her feet. At the sight of the lion he trembled with fear, especially when he called to mind Mary's words that she had never seen wild beasts in the desert. But guarding himself with the sign of the Cross, the thought came to him that the power of the one lying there would protect him and keep him unharmed. Meanwhile the lion drew nearer to him, expressing affection by every movement.

Zosimas said to the lion:

"The Great One ordered that her body was to be buried. But I am old and have not the strength to dig the grave (for I have no spade and it would take too long to go and get one), so can you carry out the work with your claws? Then we can commit to the earth the mortal temple of the saint."

While he was still speaking the lion with his front paws began to dig a hole deep enough to bury the body.

Again the elder washed the feet of the saint with his tears and calling on her to pray for all, covered the body with earth in the presence of the lion. It was as it had been, naked and uncovered by anything but the tattered cloak which had been given to her by Zosimas and with which Mary, turning away, had managed to cover part of her body. Then both departed. The lion went off into the depth of the desert like a lamb, while Zosimas returned to the monastery glorifying and blessing Christ our Lord. And on reaching the monastery he told all the brothers

[6]St. Mary died in 522 A.D.

about everything, and all marvelled on hearing of God's miracles. And with fear and love they kept the memory of the saint.

Abbot John, as St. Mary had previously told Abba Zosimas, found a number of things wrong in the monastery and got rid of them with God's help. And Saint Zosimas died in the same monastery, almost attaining the age of a hundred, and passed to eternal life. The monks kept this story without writing it down and passed it on by word of mouth to one another.

But I (adds Saint Sophronius) as soon as I heard it, wrote it down. Perhaps someone else, better informed, has already written the life of the Saint, but as far as I could, I have recorded everything, putting truth above all else. May God Who works amazing miracles and generously bestows gifts on those who turn to Him with faith, reward those who seek light for themselves in this story, who hear, read and are zealous to write it, and may He grant them the lot of blessed Mary together with all who at different times have pleased God by their pious thoughts and labours.

And let us also give glory to God, the eternal King, that He may grant us too His mercy in the day of judgment for the sake of Jesus Christ our Lord, to Whom belongs all glory, honour, dominion and adoration with the Eternal Father and the Most Holy and Life-giving Spirit, now and always, and throughout all ages. Amen.

TROPARION · TONE 8

In thee, O Mother, was exactly preserved what was according to the divine image. For thou didst take the cross and follow Christ, and by thy life, didst teach us to ignore the flesh, since it is transitory, but to care for the soul as an immortal thing. Therefore, thy spirit, St. Mary, rejoices with the Angels.

KONTAKION · TONE 4

Having escaped the fog of sin, and having illumined thy heart with the light of penitence, O glorious one, thou didst come to Christ and didst offer to Him His immaculate and holy Mother as a merciful intercessor. Hence thou hast found remission of transgressions, and with the Angels thou ever rejoicest.